To: John



# OXFORD R

## THEIR CITY • THEIR LIVES

**Rob Walters**

Contents

*To the rogues who enhance our lives*

**Acknowledgements**

Thanks to all those who have, wittingly or unwittingly, contributed to this book including:
Peter Ashby, John Dougill, Ted East, Jocelyn Paine

---

Oxford Rogues


First published 2008
Oxface Publications
28 Fairacres Road
Oxford, OX4 1TF

ISBN 978-0-9512388-3-7



The author and publishers would like to thank the following for permission to reproduce their photographs:
Oxford Mail and Times: Richard Burton (p.10), Graham Greene (p.30), Howards Marks (p.39)
Robert Maxwell (p.69), Bill Clinton (p.78).

Acknowledgement for copyright permission is gratefully made to:
The National Portrait Gallery for portraits of Lord Rochester (p.4) and Percy Shelley (p.86).
Both images © 'National Portrait Gallery, London'.
The Natural History Museum, London for the portrait of Sir Richard Burton (p.19).
Lincoln College for the portrait of Sir William Davenant (p.62). Reproduced by kind permission of the Rector and Fellows of Lincoln College, Oxford.

Colour photography © Paul Medley. White Horse © Rob Walters
Cover design and artwork: Paul Medley
Black and white photographs of Oxford by Rob Walters and Paul Medley

# Roguery in Oxford

*Farewell, farewell, dear Oxford! God bless thee, and increase thy sons in number, holiness and virtue.* - Elizabeth I (1592)

Well, Elizabeth, the sons of Oxford certainly did increase in number, but there were a few who were not so hot on the holiness or the virtue. These are the sons that you will meet in this book. They are mostly rogues in the nicest sense – as in a 'fun-loving, mischievous person, or someone who is pleasantly mischievous or frolicsome'. Mostly not in the more negative interpretations: 'a deceitful and unreliable scoundrel, a rascal', or the older meaning of rogue – 'a wandering beggar or tramp, a vagabond'.

I do not regard myself as a rogue, though others might disagree and perhaps there is something of the rogue in all of us. However, the rogues of this trail are special: they are all famous or at least infamous in some walk of life; they all have a strong connection with Oxford; and they all have a tale which must be told.

Three of the rogues were in Oxford in the seventeenth century. Celia Fiennes travelled through the city during this period and admired the beautiful buildings. However, she also noted that the college fellows 'may live very Neatly if Sober'. This was a time of great change: Oxford became the capital of England during the Civil War, and the Restoration was renowned for its liberalism and inventiveness. Two of the rogues were in the city in the nineteenth century and this, for the university, was a century divided. Concerning its early stages Thomas Hogg wrote of 'a total neglect of all learning, an unseemly turbulence, the most monstrous irregularities, open and habitual drunkenness, vice and violence...' Yet the latter part of that century saw great reforms which included the removal of religious stricture and the introduction of women. Those reforms continued apace into the twentieth century when the remaining five rogues came to the city.

So wander through the streets of Oxford – in your mind or in actuality – and meet some of the fascinating characters from its colourful past. You can follow the rogue male trail that this book creates through the map at the back of the book. You can also become a rogue assessor. Roguishness is assessed against the following criteria and is scored on a scale of 1 to 5, the higher the mark the greater the rogue:

Rogue Assessment:

| | | | | | | | |
|---|---|---|---|---|---|---|---|
| Charmer | [ ] | Womaniser | [ ] | Drinker | [ ] | Liar | [ ] |
| Entertainer | [ ] | Corrupter | [ ] | Adventurer | [ ] | Creator | [ ] |

First of all try a rogue assessment on yourself. Then do an assessment for each of the characters on the rogue male trail – see who you think was, or is, the biggest rogue in Oxford. Go to my web site **www.satin.co.uk** to see who is currently top of the rogues and, if you wish, vote for your favourite or nominate new ones.

# THE LIBERTINE
## Lord Rochester
*1647-80*

The rogue male trail commences at Wadham College, a charmingly robust early seventeenth-century building on the eastern side of Parks Road. Little has changed here since Dorothy Wadham had the place built following her husband's last wishes though it has discreetly expanded to the east with new buildings and to the south by acquisition – it owns the splendid King's Arms pub and much of the northern frontage of Holywell Street. Through all of this expansion it has become one of the largest colleges in Oxford.

During the troubled years of Cromwell's Commonwealth Christopher Wren studied at Wadham under the wardenship of John Wilkins. Robert Boyle, Robert Hooke and other scientists of the day visited them for the meetings that ultimately gave birth to the Royal Society. But these men were scientists, not rogues. The rogue whose life of debauchery began at Wadham was John Wilmot. He was an Oxfordshire man – born in Ditchley and buried in Spelsbury – and he became the second Earl of Rochester.

Why start the trail with Wilmot? Well, why not? Wadham is an excellent place to start and the King's Arms provides a convivial meeting place for rogue hunters. And if you have not heard of Rochester then this little poem might help. It is a much quoted verse that he, rather unwisely, pinned to the door of Charles II's room whilst the monarch was in residence at Christ Church:

> Here lies a great and mighty King,
> Whose promise none relied on;
> He never said a foolish thing,
> Nor ever did a wise one.

There were many others poems – but let's save those for later.

Rochester was educated initially at a school not so far from Oxford, the Burford Grammar School, where he was described as 'a model pupil'. The school still exists: it is now a comprehensive and one of the few state schools to have boarding facilities – in fact the school's boarding house is the original building in which Rochester was taught. I know this school well: both of my sons went there, though they tell me that its most famous son was never mentioned during their stay. Clearly he was not considered a suitable role model for the boys and girls of their day!

Rochester entered Oxford at the amazingly young age of twelve, becoming a 'fellow commoner' in 1660 – the year of the restoration of Charles II. He was warmly described by Anthony Wood (Oxford's Samuel Pepys) as 'thoroughly acquainted with the classic authors, both Greek and Latin; a thing very rare (if not peculiar to him) among those of his quality'.

Thus the young but brilliant Rochester came up to Oxford at a very impressionable age and in a very impressive period of our history. The king was back; the repressive years of the Commonwealth were over; and, as Anthony Wood described it, 'The world of England was perfectly mad. They [the people] were free from the chains of darkness and confusion, which the Presbyterians and the Fanatics had brought upon them.' The pubs were back in full swing; the theatres getting ready to open; Christmas could be celebrated once more; and the loyalty of those who had supported the king during the republican years was soon to be repaid.

Wadham College quad

And how would a young lad just twelve years of age fare in the rejoicing city of Oxford? Badly, I'm afraid. It is claimed that the young lord was guided into debauchery by Robert Whitehall, a fellow of Merton and considerably older than himself. Whitehall has been described as a minor poet and a great drinker, but not as a great thinker. Some claim that the pair drank at the Saracen's Head, a hostelry long since gone. According to Derek Honey, Oxford's historic pubs expert, it stood in the High Street next to the Angel Inn, also long gone. The Angel belonged to Magdalen College and was purchased by the university in the nineteenth century to allow the construction of the splendid Examination Schools – a building that many of the rogues in this book managed to avoid for one reason or another.

Besides the corrupting influence of Robert Whitehall there was at least one other man who made a great impression on the young lord: his name was James Themut. This man came to Oxford posing as a medical doctor. His practice was short lived: after a few months he rapidly made off taking with him a purse full of ill-earned money and leaving behind many dissatisfied patients. He may well have been the model for Rochester's own impersonation of a doctor in later life.

At the remarkably young age of fourteen Rochester was awarded a Master's Degree by Lord Clarendon, his uncle. Clarendon was both Lord Chancellor of England and Chancellor of Oxford University. He was also influential in Charles II's new government and in awarding the degree may well have been rewarding the son for the loyalty of the father. The first Earl of Rochester, John Wilmot's father, had aided the escape of Charles II during the Civil War and died whilst an adviser to the king in exile.

Clarendon was also an adviser to the king during the long wait for the Restoration, later earning himself a special place in the memoirs of Oxford. He wrote a great book on the Civil War, the royalties of which were donated to the University in order to construct a new building to house the Oxford University Press. That edifice, the Clarendon Building, lies just to the south of Wadham College, at the junction of Parks Road and Broad Street.

The King's Arms in Parks Road, next to Wadham College

His academic and moral education complete, Rochester needed a little rounding off. With the king's permission he embarked on a grand four-year tour of France and Italy with Sir Andrew Balfour, a distinguished botanist whose fondness for wine perhaps advanced Rochester's own. The young lord certainly had a taste for the stuff: later in life he claimed that he was permanently drunk for a period of five years!

The grand tour completed, Rochester returned to England and entered the court of Charles II where he began his career as the court libertine: poet, imbiber, womaniser, pugilist and patron of the arts. For a while he became an officer in the navy and acquitted himself well in the battles against the Dutch, showing great bravery in the thick of battle.

At court Rochester regularly disgraced himself in deed and poetry. His poems are at best risqué, and at worst pornographic. For all of that his poetry has been much admired by the likes of Graham Greene, who wrote a biography of him, and is said to be insightful and excellently composed. The more salacious poems include:

*The Imperfect Enjoyment* – about premature ejaculation
*Signor Dildoe* – 'This Signor is sound, safe, ready and dumb
As ever was candle, carrot or thumb'
*The Debauchee* – 'I send for my whore, when for fear of the clap
I dally about her, and spew in her lap'
*Sodom, or the Quintessence of Debauchery* – no explanation necessary
*A Ramble in St. James's Park* – on sexual honesty

I expect that you get the picture. One of his poems was called *A Satyre on Charles II.* It is a lampoon of the king, very earthy and not at all flattering with much mention of the king's member and its influence on his leadership. Rochester, probably in his cups, handed the king this poem in mistake for another. Charles scanned the thing with growing horror, then banished the author from his court. For all of that – or perhaps because of it – he was forgiven, returned to court, and rose to the rank of Gentleman of the Bedchamber. This amusing title may sound appropriate for a man seemingly obsessed with sex, but the position was a significant one bringing with it an intimate knowledge of the monarch's activities. It was only awarded to the king's closest friends.

One of Rochester's greatest escapades was the abduction of a lady. He began to court an heiress called Elizabeth Mallet, a highly desirable marriage partner. When he was rejected by her, he took matters into his own hands. As Elizabeth made her way home from dinner at Whitehall one evening Rochester, with a group of armed men, intercepted her carriage in Charing Cross and carried her off. She was recovered shortly afterwards, but her abductor was sent to the Tower of London for this crazy adventure. However, after just three weeks he was released having employed all of his poetic skills to petition the king for forgiveness. Less than two years later he married Elizabeth.

But Rochester was not loyal to his beautiful heiress. There were whores and there were mistresses. The most famous of the latter was Elizabeth Barry of whom it was said that 'he never loved any person so sincerely as he did Mrs. Barry'. Rochester claims that he took charge of her life, transforming her from a bit-part actress to a famed and talented player and singer. They had a child, a little girl, who was adopted by Rochester when the affair ended.

In the foetid atmosphere of Charles II's court it comes as no surprise that there were frequent quarrels, and that Rochester was right there in the midst of them. Some of these led to banishment. On one occasion he boxed Thomas Killigrew's ears in the presence of the king (Killigrew was a playwright and producer, he held a similar position to Rochester at court) and was banished once more. But the king was soon asking, 'Where is Rochester?' And to the usual response, 'You banned him sire,' he would rejoin, 'Well, bring him back, I miss the fellow.' As Graham Greene wrote in his biography of the feckless lord: 'Reflections on the King and his mistresses which cost Sir John Coventry his nose cost Rochester, time and again, no more than a few weeks banishment from Court. … Up to the last years of his life the Earl was receiving many favours from the King, whom he continued to lampoon.'

It is claimed that Rochester dearly loved his wife and children (three by his wife – Anne, Charles and Mallet – as well as one with Elizabeth Barry). One biographer describes his marriage as 'unusually happy'. That seems difficult to swallow given his uproarious lifestyle in London and his evil reputation – but these were different times. He was frequently in debt, but apparently did not take advantage of his wife's wealth to extricate himself.

Although I have found no definite record that Rochester returned to Oxford, he must surely have passed through the city on many occasions. He had family land at nearby Adderbury and the king had appointed him the Keeper and Ranger of Woodstock Park, which included a house as well as extensive grounds. Here he regularly visited his family and led the life of a country gentleman before returning to the Royal Court, the House of Lords, and the stewpots of London.

According to John Aubrey, 'he was wont to say that when he came to Brentford the Devil entered into him and never left him till he came into the Country again.'

But there were occasions when Rochester was at neither of these places, nor was he himself. He had a penchant for disguise and pretence. During one of the periods of absence he posed as an innkeeper and on others as Dr Bendo, a spoof medical doctor who specialised, surprise, surprise, in the treatment of barren women. This was the role inspired by the visit of James Themut to Oxford during Rochester's student days.

Another person who is said to have influenced Rochester's traumatic life is the philosopher Thomas Hobbes: in Anthony Wood's words 'the Court…not only debauched him but made him a perfect Hobbist.' Hobbes was another Oxford graduate, and was sometime tutor to the future Charles II during his exile in Paris. He had studied at Hertford, the college whose two halves are linked by the famous 'Bridge of Sighs' and which is barely a stone's throw from Wadham.

The most famous work by Hobbes is *Leviathan* (1651), a study of politics, morality and society which portrays the state as a giant: an artificial man composed of men (women did exist in those days but were pretty much ignored by philosophers). It was published when Rochester was just three years old. Hobbes maintained that the only control that government should exercise is the prevention of harm by one man on another. What happened outside of this was pretty much people's own business. This gives great licence to the populace, which would hold an obvious appeal for Rochester – and for many of our other rogues. Furthermore Hobbes seems to disregard religion as a source of enlightenment. He clearly regarded it as a useful tool of government, but not as a way of getting closer to God. This was revolutionary thinking in the early seventeenth century. Some say the philosopher's writing had a clear influence not just on Rochester's dissolute life but also on his poetry, in particular the poem 'Love and Life' which ends thus:

> Then talk not of inconstancy
> False hearts, and broken vows;
> If I by miracle can be
> This live-long minute true to thee,
> 'Tis all that Heaven allows.

Finally, the baseness of Rochester's lifestyle took its toll. He contracted syphilis and perhaps other sexually transmitted diseases, as well as suffering an ailing liver. His nose rotted from his face and the skin formed disgusting gummas; a wretchedness that he disguised with a false nose and a pancake mixture in order to make his last great appearance in the House of Lords to support the king.

John Wilmot, the second Earl of Rochester, libertine, poet and rogue, died at the age of thirty-three of syphilis and cirrhosis of the liver. It is claimed that he renounced atheism and converted to christianity at the very end of his life. He was buried in the crypt of the delightful parish church of Spelsbury: the parson conducting the ceremony described him as 'so great a man and so great a sinner'. Tragically his wife and son joined him there within a year.

Rochester is not highly regarded as a son of Oxford, but there is one memorial to him. It takes the form of a rather nice plaque at Wadham hidden away in the cloister-like corridor behind the hall and chapel. It describes him as both libertine and poet. The media is less circumspect: in the 2004 film *The Libertine,* Johnny Depp portrays Rochester in all his finery and filth. The film begins with a chilling close-up of Depp dressed as Lord Rochester enunciating the words, 'You will not like me'. And maybe you do not, but some did, and some still do! His admirers have included: Defoe, Tennyson, Voltaire, Goethe, Hazlitt and, of course, Graham Greene.

Perhaps the last word on Lord Rochester should go to another student of Oxford: a man called Samuel Johnson who attended Pembroke College some seventy years after our rogue's short stay at Wadham. Johnson wrote this of him: 'In a course of drunken gaiety and gross sensuality, with intervals of study perhaps yet more criminal, with an avowed contempt of decency and order, a total disregard to every moral, and a resolute denial of every religious observation, he lived worthless and useless, and blazed out his youth and health in lavish voluptuousness.'

Not much chance of being blessed by Queen Elizabeth then, Rochester! Shame on you! Yet I suspect that he would have only smiled roguishly if he had ever lived to see Johnson's character assessment. And Johnson himself could direct a kindlier, less vitriolic phrase in Rochester's direction, 'In all his works there is a sprightliness and vigour, and everywhere may be found tokens of a mind which study might have carried to excellence.' And that remark terminates the short life of John Wilmot, second Earl of Rochester: Oxford graduate, roguish poet, and loyal friend of Charles II.

Rogue Assessment:

| | | | | | | | |
|---|---|---|---|---|---|---|---|
| Charmer | [ ] | Womaniser | [ ] | Drinker | [ ] | Liar | [ ] |
| Entertainer | [ ] | Corrupter | [ ] | Adventurer | [ ] | Creator | [ ] |

**Sources**:

*Lord Rochester's Monkey, being the Life of John Wilmot, Second Earl of Rochester* by Graham Greene. The Bodley Head, 1974
*Aubrey's Brief Lives* edited by Oliver Lawson-Dick. Mandarin, 1992
*John Wilmot 2nd Earl of Rochester*. Leaflet by All Saints Church, Spelsbury
*Lives of the English Poets* by Samuel Johnson. Bernhard Tauchnitz, 1858

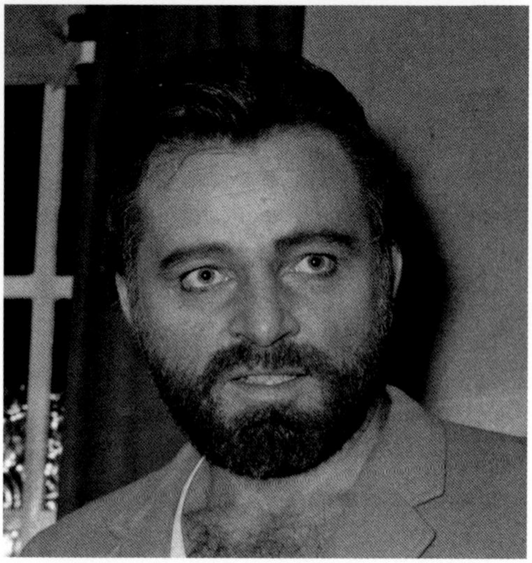

## THE ACTOR
## Richard Burton
*1925-84*

The trail continues from Wadham, south along Parks Road and then alongside the King's Arms. This has been a pub since 1607 and was the last in Oxford to have a male-only bar, a reminder that the majority of the colleges were solely for men right up until 1974 when long-established colleges such as Jesus began to accept women. Turning right at the traffic lights next to the pub provides an excellent view of the Clarendon Building. Completed in 1713 it is a sturdy, classical affair with heavy Tuscan pillars and a wide arch which pierces the whole building, giving glimpses of the Old Bodleian Library and Radcliffe Camera beyond. Originally built to house the Oxford University Press, it now serves as offices for the Bodleian. At one stage in its history it was home to the university's police force which had its cells in the cellars below. It was designed by Nicholas Hawkesmore, student and assistant to Christopher Wren who first turned his hand to architecture in Oxford by completing the building next door: the Sheldonian Theatre.

With its protective curve of bearded emperors, the Sheldonian is a fine building, definitely one of the sights of Oxford and one which many of our rogues must have visited. Based loosely on the Theatre of Marcellus in Rome, it has the largest unsupported ceiling of its time: this is a clever design implemented by Wren – the ceiling is suspended from above. Building began in 1664, just after Rochester left Oxford for his European tour, and it was opened in 1669. The main business that is conducted here is the welcoming of new students into the University of Oxford (matriculation), and the awarding of degrees for those who stay the course. A seemingly round building, it is actually D-shaped with a decorative flat front facing the Divinity School where students don their gowns in readiness for the graduation ceremony.

Next door again is the old Ashmolean Museum, now the fascinating Museum of the History of Science. Not a place for rogues perhaps, though here you can see the stone that Elizabeth I's astrologer, Doctor Dee, used in communicating with angels. I would not suggest that Dee was a rogue, far from it. But Edward Kelly, his prime means of communicating with the spirits, almost certainly was. Kelly was Dee's scryer, a medium through whom Dee could communicate with the spiritual world. As their relationship advanced Kelly reported that he had received a message from the angels that they must share everything – including their wives. How convenient for Kelly!

Opposite the museum is the famous Blackwell's bookshop – the original. Back in 1925 a young lady named Vivien Dayrell-Browning worked here as an intern. We will hear more of her later as the first love, and lifetime wife, of Graham Greene. Half-sunken below the bookshop is the White Horse pub. Tiny, awkward, but loveable, this is the pub where Richard Burton the actor, Sir Richard Burton the explorer and Howard Marks the cannabis smuggler met in the spring of 2003. Well not exactly, after all two of them were dead at the time. This meeting was between three 'think-alikes': friends of mine who agreed to act the part of each character whilst I paid for the beer and recorded their conversation – a memorable and inspirational evening.

The Sheldonian Theatre

Next to the History of Science Museum is Exeter College where we meet our next rogue – Richard Burton. Exeter is a very ancient college, the fourth oldest if we exclude St Edmund's Hall. It was founded in 1314 and, though most of what you see on the outside is much later than this, Palmer's Tower in the northeast corner of the front quadrangle dates from 1432. This college seems to attract writers and artists, including J.R.R. Tolkien, William Morris and Edward Burne-Jones, to name just a few. The door between the two distinct nineteenth-century ranges fronting Broad Street is used solely for vehicular access and normally remains closed. The main entrance actually lies in Turl Street, facing out towards Jesus College on the other side of the road. It is through this entrance that Richard Burton arrived in April of 1944. He was a Welshman with attitude and the son of a coal miner; a handsome young man with a striking face coarsened by acne. He was already a budding actor having travelled around England with Emlyn Williams in a play entitled *The Druid's Rest* (1944). Born Richard Jenkins, he changed his name to Burton as a teenager. In this account, partly to avoid confusion with the next rogue (who was actually born Richard Burton) we will call him Richard.

Richard came to Oxford for a special, six-month wartime course. He was an RAF cadet, not an undergraduate. He attended Oxford to receive a taste of university life with the opportunity to return to complete a degree after the war. Many young men were at Oxford for this reason during wartime, an odd arrangement but presumably it made some sense at the time. In fact Richard did not return to complete his degree, though he did revisit Oxford many times during his acting career. Whilst at the university he attended lectures in English literature which were slotted in between service parades and military classes. He also began to learn Italian, though where this fitted into his later life I do not know. Most importantly he found a lot of time for drama: real-life drama and that performed on the stage.

The man who, without doubt, had the most influence on Richard's career at Oxford was Professor Nevill Coghill, at that time a Fellow of Exeter and later Merton Professor of English. He is best known for his verse translation of Chaucer's *Canterbury Tales* into modern English. This man was key to Richard's two appearances in Oxford theatres and pivotal in determining his future. In his private records Nevill Coghill wrote, 'I have only had two men of genius to teach – W.H. Auden and Richard Burton. When they happen one cannot mistake them.'

Nevill Coghill's rooms at Exeter were a mess. In the 1940s a student wrote this description for a student magazine called the *Cherwell*: 'Books all over the chairs and couches, designs for sets on the floor – and their tall, tough, typically Irish tenant – grizzled somewhat at the temples now, with a pullover to match – stepping over everything with a brontosauric grace in his anxiety to find you a cigarette…'

Exeter College as seen from Broad Street

Coghill kept good company, at one time being identified with the Inklings, a group of writers which included C.S. Lewis and J.R.R Tolkien. The Inklings met at the Eagle and Child public house in St Giles, not far from the current Playhouse Theatre in which Richard later performed with Elizabeth Taylor.

When Richard arrived at Exeter College Nevill Coghill was looking after the Oxford University Dramatic Society, and preparations were already well advanced for a performance of Shakespeare's *Measure for Measure* in the cloisters of Christ Church. Richard sought out Nevill to ask for a part in the play, but all the roles were filled. However, during the meeting Richard recited the Hamlet soliloquy 'To be or not to be…' Nevill was impressed and decided to give him the job of understudying the lead part: that of Angelo, then allocated to Hallam Fordham. Richard attended rehearsals regularly and somehow he inherited the part: either by Welsh wizardry, or by giving Hallam a nervous breakdown, or, as Nevill Coghill has it, because Hallam was posted away from Oxford before the play began.

Richard took the opportunity to perform in his first ever Shakespearean play very seriously. He asked Phillip Burton, his 'adopted father', to come to Oxford and together they went through Angelo's lines, word by word, working well into the small hours. Philip stayed at Exeter College overnight and saw the show the next day. Though the reviews were mixed, the appearance as Angelo proved a breakthrough for Richard. An influential London theatre promoter called Hugh 'Binkie' Beaumont was in the audience and, after the performance, he asked Richard if he wished to be a professional. The young actor said that he wasn't sure. Binkie gave him a card and told him to call at his London office whenever he was ready to begin an acting career. And so the door to his future had opened.

Phillip Burton tells a story about the play's first night which has entered into Oxford mythology. After the performance of *Measure for Measure* Richard went to a party, whereas Phillip returned to the college. Phillip waited many hours for his protégé to return. When he did finally arrive, his trousers were torn and his legs bloodied. Richard explained that the college gates were locked when he finally got back so he had climbed over 'a wall – or was it a fence'. A likely tale!

There are stories of heavy beer drinking during Richard's stay in Oxford. He claimed that he could drink the sconce, two and half pints of beer, in ten seconds and that this was a record. It probably was in those days, though it was Bob Hawke, later Prime Minister of Australia, who entered the Guinness Book of Records for his speedy sinking of the sconce. Records aside, the young man gained the title 'Beer Burton' during his stay in Oxford so he must have drunk some. When Cis, his older sister and effective stepmother, visited him she was strongly impressed by the beauty of the colleges. However, her tour of the joys of Oxford was interrupted when one of Richard's friends mentioned the possibility of going for a pint later. Cis, a teetotaller, said,
'What? Beer? In a place like this?'
'Well, we do have the occasional drink,' Richard confessed with a roguish smile.

He had two regular drinking companions: one from his own college, a West Countryman called Conway, and another whom he had met whilst performing *Measure for Measure* – John Wain who played Claudio. Conway seems to have left little trace but John Wain became a writer (of plays, poetry, fiction and biography) and Professor of Poetry at Oxford. Perhaps he represents what Richard might have been had his life taken a different direction. Wain's memoirs give a rare insight into Richard Burton at Oxford. He talks for instance of Richard's 'electrifying' performance in the play and that 'we recognised him as a better actor than the rest of us, though the enormous difference between us did not open out till later.'

Conway, the other drinking companion, knew all the words to popular songs such as *Any Old Iron*, and the others joined him in singing as they strolled between pubs. Richard taught John the basics of bar billiards, but the evenings were mostly filled with beer and talk. Richard did most of the talking: pontificating about Wales, about his acting, about rugby, and about preachers. John remembered tales of a rugby player who killed himself as he ran headfirst into the goal post, and of preachers who could bring a congregation to tears. John's view was that Richard was not a noisy man in company, not the life and soul of the party type, but he did have a tendency to slip into recitation after a few pints. Once, at a party in Ship Street, he suddenly stood up and walked to the bookcase. He removed a bible and quickly found II Samuel 18 and read aloud the account of the death of Absalom and the lamentation of David. Afterwards he simply slipped back into the party, no doubt leaving a strong impression on the stunned set of guests. John wrote later of 'the voice, the magnetic stillness of his body as he spoke'.

It is clear that John Wain looked up to Richard as an older, more experienced man – though they were actually close in age. He asked the Welshman what to 'use' in sex, but Richard just shrugged and said, 'I never use anything.' And John wondered how he got away with it – low fertility or lack of success? One night they were playing bar billiards together, it was near to closing time and they had just inserted a 'sixpence or tanner' into the slot which provided a certain duration of play. Soon the landlord was harrying them to leave and John was all for laying down the cues and departing. But Richard stood his ground saying to the landlord, 'We've got to get our tanner's worth, old man.'

Naturally, there were associations with women. However, the only recorded incident that I have discovered was not fruitful. Nina Bawden, who became a novelist, was at Somerville whilst Richard was at Exeter. They met at a dance and he later called at the college to 'take her to tea'. He was limping on arrival, climbing over 'that wall – or was it a fence' at Exeter again no doubt, but Nina noticed that the limp faded as they walked to the teashop. This teashop, according to someone who was at Somerville at the time, must have been Fullers in the Cornmarket which has long gone. There Richard tried to persuade Nina to go to London for the weekend – suggesting that they could stay at Emlyn Williams's house. She was not impressed; in fact she doubted that he knew anyone so famous, though she did think that he looked older than his years because of the pockmarks and boils that scarred his young face.

Richard seems to have had some problems with sex at this time, but said that he met an older woman in Oxford who 'sorted him out about all that. No trouble ever since.' What the trouble was we shall never know for sure, but we can guess.

Richard's natural father was not impressed by his son's attendance at Oxford. According to brother Dai, their father said that he should much better have distinguished himself by playing rugby for Wales – you can't win them all! Dai also spoke of the contrast between the bleakness of their origins and the grandeur of the university with its inspiring college buildings. But what did Richard himself think of Oxford? Nearly thirty years after his arrival he said, 'I fell in love with it and have remained in love with it. If I get the chance, I go back there. It had, and still has, a curious, almost mystic impact on me.' He did indeed return many times to the city, both as a famous actor and as a humble academic.

After that first stay as a student Richard left the city brimming with confidence, a successful professional performance and a lead Shakespearean part already under his belt. He had escaped the tyranny of the Welsh valleys without losing his love of South Wales or his Welshness. He had rubbed shoulders with the toffs of Oxford and come out on top. He had won the admiration of the key dramatic don in Oxford and had an offer of work from the top theatre entrepreneur in London. Life was good, the world was his oyster, but now he was off to train for war. Mercifully that war was drawing to a close and Richard did not see active service, though he did spend time in Canada as part of his Royal Air Force training.

Richard's career blossomed quickly after his demobilisation. He cashed in on his performance as Angelo at Christ Church, landing himself a retainer with Binkie Beaumont's theatre company. Films quickly followed and then, the glittering prize, a contract in Hollywood. He liked the place and mostly it liked him – but not for long. He soon returned to Britain – to the Old Vic to play Hamlet and to earn his credentials as a professional Shakespearean actor. Perhaps the most famous film of his Hollywood era was *The Robe* (1953), in which he plays tribune Marcellus Gallio opposite Jean Simmonds's Diana. This was a big film, on a big topic. It encompasses the crucifixion, the coming to power of Caligula and the rise of christianity in the Roman Empire. Though the film brought him 'more money than he thought there was in the world', he did not have a high opinion of it. And, during his stay in Hollywood, his roguish side became more apparent. He drank and he womanised. Lauren Bacall, a supporter of Richard's wife Sybil, said that 'People did not like his going around the town with one after the other.'

Throughout his career Richard regularly returned to his roots. Already famous, he visited his hometown on one occasion to play rugby against a neighbouring village. In the pub after the game he hoped for some complimentary comment on his play, but none came. Then two of the miners in the opposing team asked Richard to come outside with them. He went, expecting some opinion concerning his rugby. But they said nothing at all. They led him to the toilet and, having consumed plenty of beer, all had a pee. This was done in silence, and still nothing was said as they re-entered the pub. Here at last Richard could bear it no more – he asked them what it was all about, why had they asked him to join them but not said a word. There was a long pause then one of them hesitantly replied, 'We jest wanted to tell our mam that we had passed water with Richard Burton.'

At the beginning of the 1960s Richard made a surprising move: he appeared in a Broadway musical called *Camelot*, playing King Arthur opposite co-star Julie Andrews. Interestingly there is a slim, but important, link between Arthur and Oxford. The mythical king primarily owes his existence to Geoffrey of Monmouth's book on the *History of the Kings of England* (c.1136). The historian was a member of the long-lost St George's College, which was located within the walls of Oxford's castle and was the probable seed corn of Oxford University.

*Camelot* had a lengthy and successful run which gave Richard a large income. He set up 'Burton's Bar' in his dressing room and was visited by the rich and the famous. His drinking reached new heights. For a bet he once drank a whole bottle of vodka in the afternoon performance and another during the evening performance. He asked Julie Andrews, an unknowing arbiter, how his acting had been that day. 'A little better than usual,' she said!

Sybil, Richard's first wife, was a girl from the Welsh valleys. She is usually portrayed as a homely, supportive, long-suffering wife who was loving and loyal right up until the moment that Richard met the woman who was to change his life. That woman was Elizabeth Taylor.

His first reaction to the world-famous actress was dislike – he referred to her as 'Miss Tits'. But she fell for him one day as he struggled to perform his part on the film set of *Cleopatra* (1963) in Italy whilst in a weak and vulnerable state following a St David's day binge. They fell in love. Fell in love deeply and, it seemed, irretrievably. Though Taylor was bluntly truthful about her feelings to her husband, Eddie Fisher, Richard was terrified of losing Sybil, his children and, in all probability, the whole of the Welsh family. They all liked Sybil.

It was the most publicised of affairs, and it occurred in the twentieth century's most morally turbulent decade. But these two were not 'children of the 60s'. She was in her early thirties and already four times married; he was in his late thirties with a long-term marriage and two children. Sybil must have forgiven him many previous indiscretions; it is not really possible that she did not know of them. But this affair ('El Scandale' as Richard called it), this Elizabeth Taylor thing, this was something different. Elizabeth wanted him entirely, an affair was not enough – and she usually got what she wanted. Both women attempted suicide: Sybil perhaps to escape, Elizabeth to get her man. Richard was virtually isolated as friends and family rushed to Sybil's support. Phillip Burton tried to talk sense to him with the result that no words passed between them for the following two years. Even Ivor, the trusted brother who accompanied Richard everywhere, abandoned him – it is said that they almost came to blows. Emlyn Williams went to Rome in an attempt to save the situation. It was unsaveable: Burton and Taylor had become an inseparable item. And so this world-famous partnership began, amidst the detritus of two previous partnerships and their associated goods, chattels, children, dogs and entourages. Within two years the divorces had been arranged, Richard had devolved most of his fortune onto Sybil and their children, and the world's most photographed couple finally married in 1964.

One of the most powerful films that they made together was *Who's Afraid of Virginia Woolf* (1966), and it was soon after its completion that Richard brought his new wife to Oxford. A return for him and a first look for her. He had come to play Doctor Faustus with Elizabeth as Helen of Troy. The play was Nevill Coghill's retirement production, and he was using it to raise money for the stage in Oxford. Richard's participation represented the repayment of a great debt; it was Nevill Coghill who had given him a start in serious stage performance over twenty years before.

The Burtons made no charge for their performance, but there were problems. First the couple had to postpone for a week just as bookings for the play began. Then there was little time left for rehearsals. Minor things did not work. Elizabeth's role was a non-speaking one; she simply had to appear at certain points in the play and look beautiful. A special trapdoor and lift had been constructed for her appearances but in the event she was 'less sylph-like than had been supposed' so the less impressive device of an entry through clouds of dry ice was employed. And on the first night an over-enthusiastic application of dry ice meant that only her feet could be seen!

The couple stayed at the Randolph Hotel, Oxford's best, which is conveniently placed next door to the Playhouse where the play was performed. It is a mark of the couple's popularity that a special rear entry was constructed from the hotel's car park so that they could get to their dressing room without risking the crowds in Beaumont Street.

The first night was a disaster. Seats were wrongly allocated, a whole section of the audience arrived late and technical problems delayed the start. Richard appeared to be nervous and had difficulty with his lines. The student cast caught his nervousness and missed their verbal cues. But as the week progressed it got better. Nonetheless the performance was hammered by some critics, who gave no leeway to the fact that it was a predominantly amateur production and a charity fundraiser. One lady who was there and still resides in Oxford told me that Richard was a disappointment for her, 'looking and sounding like a testy little Welsh schoolmaster'. Others, including Nevill Coghill of course, praised the performance. In any event Richard had returned to Oxford as a hero.

Don Chapman, theatre critic for the local paper, went to see the play twice and remembers it very well. On one occasion he had two London reporters in front of him: they were nuisances. They didn't know the play but were keen to see Taylor playing the most beautiful woman in the world since at that time she really *was* considered the most beautiful woman in the world. But she did not appear until late in the play and they grew increasingly fidgety as the danger of missing their deadline increased. In Don's view it was an outstanding production and the story about Elizabeth and the lift is, he says, 'cobblers' for he recalls seeing her rise through the floor and into the dry ice in both performances that he attended. In his view the last speech of Marlowe's play is the key moment, and Richard excelled himself in delivering it.

The Burton Taylor Studio

A film of the play followed, financed by the Burtons and shot in Rome together with the original actors. Unfortunately the film was not a success and the play itself made very little money for the appeal fund. As Elizabeth said, 'We might as well have played Hollywood and let the profs have whatever we earned.' Finally Richard offered Nevill Coghill £100,000 of his own money and promised to help extract donations from Aristotle Onassis and other wealthy friends. The money took a long time to arrive, but arrive it did and was used to build the little Burton Taylor Studio which now overlooks Gloucester Green in the centre of the city.

There were to be other links with Oxford. Sometime during the sumptuous celebration of Elizabeth's fortieth birthday Francis Warner of St Peter's College took Richard aside to whisper in his ear. He spoke of the possibility of a fellowship at the college. The fellowship was later confirmed 'by order of the Queen'. Richard was clearly very proud to receive this honour, though just a little puzzled. He said that it gave him subtle satisfaction and he rated it a greater achievement than a knighthood. After all, many actors had become 'Sirs' but he believed himself the first to gain a fellowship at Oxford.

Sometime after this Richard's life was shattered by the mysterious death of his elder brother, Ivor. He began to drink with a vengeance and the eight-year period of loyalty to Elizabeth was squandered on the set of the film *Bluebeard* (1972). The horror film was not a success – it was not even frightening – though the girls murdered by Richard's character were nice to look at. And so, in a combination of booze and beards, the famous Burton-Taylor marriage began to flounder.

But all was not entirely gloom and despondency. He did manage a visit to Oxford to take up Francis Warner's offer of the fellowship. He stayed at the house of a friend, Simon Hornby, at Pusey in Oxfordshire and taught literature to undergraduates for a few weeks. He was said to be a quirky, yet inspiring, teacher. He had planned to stay, to write, to become an academic (even under the crushingly punitive threat of British taxation), but he was unsettled and was soon on the way back to Yugoslavia to finish a film on Tito. Another dream, becoming an Oxford don, had been briefly realised, but he was now driven by other forces. The death of Ivor seemed to have placed the devil in the driving seat and the path was set for the inevitable divorce which finally occurred in 1974, after ten years of marriage.

However, after flings with Princess Elizabeth of Yugoslavia and others, Richard got together with Elizabeth Taylor again in Geneva. They fell in love once more, dumped their partners, and re-married in October 1975 in Botswana. One month later he brought his new wife back to Oxford, to visit Francis Warner at St. Peter's. He gave a seminar to students in the morning and took Elizabeth to a 'Welcome Home' party at St Peter's in the evening. Local journalist Christopher Gray was there and whilst interviewing Richard was interrupted by the intrusive microphone of Libby Purves, then working for BBC Radio Oxford. The Welshman dealt with her in a way most people will warm to: 'Would you mind waiting your turn,' he said, 'Can't you see I'm talking to *this* gentleman.'

The second marriage did not last, 'can't live without, can't live with' still dominated their lives, and by August of the following year they were divorced again: this time for good. There were other marriages and other films, but Richard's life was in decline; alcohol was an ongoing problem and Richard Burton, actor, rogue and Oxford don, died at his home at Céligny, Switzerland in 1984 having just completed the film of George Orwell's book – *1984*!

Rogue Assessment:

| | | | | | | | |
|---|---|---|---|---|---|---|---|
| Charmer | [ ] | Womaniser | [ ] | Drinker | [ ] | Liar | [ ] |
| Entertainer | [ ] | Corrupter | [ ] | Adventurer | [ ] | Creator | [ ] |

Sources:

*Dear Shadows: Portraits from Memory* by John Wain. John Murray, 1986
*OUDS: A Centenary of the Oxford University Dramatic Society* by Humphrey Carpenter. Oxford University Press, 1985
*Richard and Phillip: The Burtons* by Phillip Burton. Peter Owen Publishers, 1992
*Richard Burton: A Brother Remembered* by David Jenkins. Century, 1993
*Richard Burton: 1925-1984* by Paul Ferris. NEL Books, 1984
*Rich: The Life of Richard Burton* by Melvyn Bragg. Coronet Books, 1988

# THE EXPLORER
## Sir Richard Burton
*1821-1890*

The next stop on the trail is just opposite the Broad Street frontage of Exeter College. It is quite possible that William Morris (of Pre-Raphaelite fame) lived in one of the nineteenth-century ranges of Exeter that face the Broad and overlook the front quad of Trinity College. In any event it was his efforts that led to the retention of those curiously misplaced Cotswold-roofed cottages that block the view into Trinity's wonderful front gardens. Squatting fearfully in front of Trinity's elegant classical chapel and the sumptuous president's lodging, they are framed by Balliol's neo-gothic frontage on one side and the solidity of Kettle Hall on the other. Poor things, sometimes I wish that I could secretly remove them to nearby Eynsham where they would be much happier.

Trinity is that strange thing – the college reborn. It shares this peculiarity with its neighbour, St John's, and with Worcester. All had been monastic colleges under another name and age. Durham College, suppressed during the reign of Henry VIII, was refounded as Trinity in 1555 by Thomas Pope. In addition to its frontage on the Broad it makes a gracious appearance in Parks Road; here the garden quad peers over a long bisected lawn through the famous blue gates and on towards Wadham on the right. It also slips almost unnoticed into Magdalen Street near the Martyrs' Memorial. It is a college that is full of surprises – from its delightful gothic-vaulted bar beneath the dining hall, to the wild woodland alongside the lawns, to the strangely named Cumberbatch Quad with its bizarre assemblage of buildings spanning six centuries.

The college would seem shockingly changed if our next rogue, Sir Richard Burton, were to return for a viewing. He entered the college in 1840, some forty years before T.G. Jackson tackled the modernisation of the front quad. In his day there were just eighty-seven people living in the place (including servants, fellows, scholars and students).

There may be some confusion here, the rogue we are now describing is *Sir* Richard Burton, the explorer, anthropologist, writer, and translator of sex manuals – a very different man from our previous rogue, Richard Burton the actor, who lived in a very different age. We will address Sir Richard in the same manner that his friends would have done in the rather formal era of the nineteenth century: we will call him Burton.

Burton entered Oxford with attitude and he certainly came to the place by an unusual route: none of the usual prep school and public school training for him. Burton's family had aristocratic ancestry but little money. His father was an officer in Duke Wellington's army, forcibly retired on half pay. The family had just sufficient funds to travel as affluent gypsies but insufficient to stay in one place and live as kings. In this way the young Burton had travelled the world, or at least much of Europe. He had seen and experienced many things that the other freshers could barely imagine. He was probably a pain in the backside to many of them.

Before entering Trinity College he was placed with a pair of Oxford tutors whose job it was to groom him for the university. They did not seem particularly successful in their work even though, in their favour, they did try to persuade him to remove the large, flamboyant moustache of which he was particularly proud. But he would not shave it off, regardless of the fact that moustaches were against the rules.

Trinity cottages

Within hours of entering the college one of the other new students had the effrontery to laugh at Burton's exceptional whiskers and the unfortunate fresher was immediately challenged to a duel! Issuing challenges of this kind was the sort of behaviour he had grown used to in his travelling teens, but we can only imagine the reaction of the poor student so challenged. Suddenly things had escalated from laughing at a funny moustache to a threat upon his life. Needless to say he did not accept the challenge, causing Burton to conclude that he was surrounded by 'the sons of grocers rather than gentlemen'! Quite a start to life at the university.

Burton was admitted as a 'commoner of the lower orders'. This would distinguish him from the 'gentlemen commoners' who paid higher fees, did less work, and wore special gowns and hats. Gentlemen commoners were the sons of the rich, and Burton – neither grocer nor gentleman – derided them.

From his room Burton looked towards Balliol College and the garden of Dr Jenkins, the master of that college. He later admitted to a grudging respect for this gentleman, but at the time he certainly did not show any. On one occasion he abseiled down into the master's garden and replaced the prize herbaceous border with 'great staring marigolds'! Good studentish fun I suppose. But generally Burton was no prankster; he was dedicated to swordplay and spent his spare time practising fencing together with a little rowing and occasionally shooting the college rooks.

It is clear that Burton did not much like the university. In particular he did not like the lectures, which he regarded as two hours wasted every day and merely provided to put pounds in the pockets of the 'droning dons'. Though he quickly established a reputation for drinking, he did not like the heavy beer which was consumed in large quantity at colleges like Brasenose. He complained that the Bodleian Library closed at three because no lights were allowed. He also didn't like the Radcliffe Camera reading room because it was damp in the wet season, stuffy in summer and 'like the cave of Aeolus in windy weather'. This typically Burtonesque simile demonstrates the learning that he had acquired in spite of, or perhaps because of, his strange upbringing. If like me you have no idea who Aeolus was, I will save you the trouble of looking him up – he was the keeper of the four winds in Greek Mythology.

Burton did not care for the city of Oxford either: in common with many people he found the climate unhealthy, describing it as 'damp air charged with marsh gases and bacteria'. He had a lifelong belief in the relationship between climate and character, claiming that the miserable atmosphere of Oxford was the reason why, unlike Cambridge, the place had not produced a Newton or a Darwin. It is, of course, true that Oxford is a damp place. It is low-lying and at the confluence of two great rivers, the Cherwell and the Thames, the latter of which Burton called 'a mere moat'! It is also true that the climate does produce depression in some – though not all.

Something that particularly annoyed Burton was the bells! He complained that they rang at all hours, often unconnected with any religious activity. This is true. The great bell in Christ Church's Tom Tower, for instance, rings 101 times at just after nine every evening. This is a tradition that dates back to when Wren first built the tower. At that time there were 101 students in the place and the bell called them to their beds. Most people like the sound but Burton did not, and Trinity is within easy earshot of Christ Church. However, he managed to solve the problem by plugging his ears with cotton wool soaked in glycerine.

At first Burton worked assiduously, devoting twelve hours each day to his Latin and Greek. But he could not, or would not, dance to the Oxford tune. He applied for a scholarship at University College, but was rejected because he spoke Latin and Greek in the modern way; he knew them as living languages from his travels. At the time Latin was spoken in a peculiar manner at the university, a manner which dated back to the Reformation and the break with Rome. Burton would not accept this odd way of speaking and committed the sin of arguing with his examiners, an argument that could never be won. It is odd to recall that Burton had been educated by an Oxford graduate. His travelling tutor, a man called Du Pré from Exeter College, should surely have apprised him of the strange way that the two ancient languages were spoken at the university?

Losing the University College scholarship grated against Burton's steely spirit and he effectively abandoned formal study at this point, dedicating himself to his own pursuits and to the study of Arabic. In the latter he was helped by an Arabist, Don Pascual de Gayangos – who first taught Burton that Arabic was read from right to left. He adopted his own method of learning, one which proved very successful and which he used extensively in later life as he wrestled with other languages. Here is an indication of his approach in his own words:

> I got a simple grammar and vocabulary, marked out the forms and words which I knew were absolutely necessary, and learnt them by heart. ... I never worked more than a quarter of an hour at a time, for after that the brain lost its freshness. After learning some

> three hundred words, easily done in a week, I stumbled through some easy book-work and underlined every word that I wished to recollect. ... Having finished my volume, I then carefully worked up the grammar minutiae, and I then chose some other book whose subject most interested me. The neck of the language was now broken, and progress was rapid. If I came across a new sound, like the Arabic Ghayn, I trained my tongue to it by repeating it so many thousand times a day. When I read, I invariably read out loud, so that the ear might aid memory. I was delighted with the most difficult characters, Chinese and Cuneiform, because I felt that they impressed themselves more strongly upon the eye than the eternal Roman letters.

Though generally critical of Oxford, there was something that Burton did like: the dogs. He was greatly taken by a local breed of bull terrier, describing it as having a 'beautiful build'. He purchased a fine example which he paraded around the city. One of his regular walks was to Bagley Woods where he visited a pretty gypsy girl called Selina. The biographies are at odds about the reason for these visits: some claim that Selina told his fortune, others that she dispensed favours to young gentlemen – a lovely phrase which mentally transforms a whore into a white-coated figure who stands alluringly behind the counter in Boots. However, there is general agreement that this was the start of Burton's long-term interest in the gypsy race, and I guess the dog enjoyed the walks.

In addition to Selina and the bull terrier, Burton had other friends – and one can always know a person by his friends. He was close to Archibald MacLaren and there is an obvious connection here: MacLaren was a fencing master who ran a gymnasium in Oxford. A much more famous associate was Tom Hughes, then studying at Oriel and later to be the author of *Tom Brown's Schooldays* (1857) and its sequel, *Tom Brown at Oxford* (1861). However, Burton's best friend, the man destined to be a lifelong supporter, was Alfred Bates Richards. He was studying at the neighbouring college of Exeter and afterwards became a poet and a playwright, also the editor of the *Sunday Telegraph* and of the *Morning Advertiser*. Richards' most famous observation of his friend is this: 'I am sure, though Burton was brilliant, rather wild, and very popular, none of us foresaw his future greatness, nor knew what a treasure we had amongst us.'

Richards was a year older than Burton and obtained his degree in 1841, after which he published an anonymous denunciation of abuses in the university entitled *Oxford Unmasked.* Through this we can sense a kindred spirit with Burton, something that may well have provided the basis for their friendship. He was said to be a man of splendid physique. Tall and strong, he defeated everyone at boxing, including Burton, but the latter was master when it came to the sword. Richards would have known his friend as 'Ruffian Dick' after a couple of well-known pugilists of those days who were called 'Old Ruffian' and 'Young Ruffian'. The name suited him and stuck with him for much of his life. And what a life that was!

During his first long vacation Burton tried desperately to persuade his father that academia was not for him – he wanted to be a soldier. But his father was unmoved – he wanted his son to enter the church. And so Burton returned grudgingly to Oxford where he went out of his way to strain to the utmost the harness of discipline imposed by the university. He made unflattering sketches of the dons and circulated them; he gave wild parties; he wrote insulting verse about the senior members of the university; and he continued to access the favours dispensed in Bagley Wood.

Trinity College

Students were forbidden the use of tandems (a carriage with two horses in line) at this time, and travel was entirely forbidden on Sundays. Burton, however, made a point of riding to the railway station in just that way and on that very day of the week. But all of this failed to attract the attention he desired. Finally in April 1842 he found a more advanced transgression with which to goad his tutors. That year the undergraduates had been specifically barred from attending the Oxford races, though many were keen to do so because a popular steeplechaser called 'Oliver' was running. Ignoring the ban, Burton joined a party of race-going students who set off from Worcester College – in tandems, of course. The miscreants were observed and reported.

The next day they were called to account. All were contrite except Burton who argued that they had done nothing wrong and that young men should not be treated as children. Consequently the others were rusticated (sent down for a while) and he himself was expelled. He left Oxford 'stung with a sense of injustice and in style'. He and a fellow miscreant, Anderson of Oriel College, made a theatrical exit – naturally enough choosing to travel by tandem. First they had their carriage plough a course through the finest flower beds at Trinity and then gallop down the High with Burton blowing on a long tin trumpet and throwing kisses to the shop girls as he made his departure towards London.

This is a nice picture, but we know from his writings that there was a tinge of regret behind the bravado, and that he would return to the city later in life. On reaching London he told his aunt that he had been awarded a double first and given an early release from the university! The claim caused some short-lived celebration, but the deception was soon unmasked by those with knowledge of academic processes.

The prodigal son's reunion with his father following his ejection from Oxford was tempered by news from the East. The terrible massacre of British troops and their followers by the Afghans enraged his father so much that he agreed to buy his son a commission in the Bombay Army: Burton became a soldier of the British East India Company. In India he hoped to see active service and to distinguish himself by 'getting a flesh wound, cutting down a brace of natives'. But this strange ambition was not to be; he regularly applied for posts that might put him at the front but, for one reason or another, he did not get the opportunity to fight.

An alternative path was through languages and, having been denied the chance to prove himself in service, he fell back upon the study of tongues. He had already taught himself some Hindustani. In India he improved on this and showed himself its master during an examination less than one year after his arrival. He then moved on to Gujarti, then to Marathi, then to other Indian languages, even extending to Turkish and Persian, that 'most elegant of Oriental languages'. Later in life he became one of the greatest linguists of his time, mastering twenty-five languages in all and, if dialects are included, reaching an incredible forty!

Trinity College from Parks Road

Burton the linguist then evolved into an anthropologist. He was appointed to the post of Assistant of the Survey by the Governor of Sind and began to 'look with interest upon the desolation around'. He read all that he could on the area, which was little, and then began his wanderings. Most of the next five years were occupied with the 'Sind Canal Survey', and this led to systematic study of the Sindian people, their manners and their tongue. To collect material for his studies he disguised himself as a Persian merchant, the first of many disguises. The studies were to result in his first books and were the beginning of a career that revolved around observation of local people.

During his stay in India he became a keen collector of Oriental manuscripts and an enthusiastic observer of native customs. He wrote either directly or indirectly of three 'love affairs' that occurred during his stay in India. The first has little to do with love since it concerns a commercial relationship. In those times it was fairly conventional to take a temporary wife, a local woman referred to as a BúBú or coloured sister. This lady acted as a sexual partner and ruled the British officer's home. There is a suggestion by some that Burton could not satisfy his BúBú and that this laid the foundations for his later misogynism.

The second Indian affair is much more fanciful. It is claimed that whilst convalescing in Pangim, Goa, Burton fell in love with a beautiful nun. She requited his love and they secretly agreed to her abduction from the nunnery. In the accounts of this story Burton steals his love away in the depth of the night with the help of a hired accomplice and a Portuguese guide. But the heist went terribly awry – the wrong nun was taken. The ugly and irritable prioress was stolen instead. She was abandoned on the seashore whilst Burton and his team made their escape.

In the third affair Burton falls in love with a beautiful Persian girl at a camel caravan stopover. The story varies, but in one version he writes a love-lorn letter to her. She replies by asking if he is a white doctor and, if so, could he recommend some medicine for her? Burton concocts a mixture of gin, sugar and Eau de Cologne. It is delivered, but we do not know the result of the treatment since soon afterwards she departs – her beautiful face covered by a burka. In a version of the story written by his niece the affair develops a little further, but the Persian beauty then dies – which is not surprising if the lady had been taking Burton's prescription of perfumed and sugary gin! However, we will never know the truth. His niece claims that this was her uncle's one true love, and all that followed paled before it.

In 1848 Burton returned to Sind and it was there that he became a Sufi master. This is an interesting development in a man who generally rejected religion – certainly orthodox religion. In later life Burton is described by Thomas Wright as half-Sufi, half-agnostic. I do not think it is realistic to be half committed to either of these disciplines, a little like being half-pregnant, but the description has an endearing veracity.

In Sind Burton worked for Sir Charles Napier, an overbearing military ruler who spotted his fluency in Indian languages and employed him to infiltrate the locals and supply intelligence. This Burton did by adopting another disguise, introducing himself as a part-Arab, part-Iranian merchant. Local people were unlikely to spot any language problems; after all, what would we expect a part-German, part-French person to sound like in English? The disguise worked well and enabled Burton to pick up a good deal of local information.

One job that Burton was given was particularly tricky – and affected his subsequent career. He had to infiltrate the three male brothels in Karachi which were suspected of corrupting local troops. He agreed to investigate, but only on the basis that the report was not shared with those at head office in Bombay. He suspected that if they got sight of it they might conclude that Burton himself was gay which, in mid nineteenth-century Victorian Britain, was a career killer. The report was completed and Napier used it as the basis for destroying the brothels. True to his word, he did not send it to Bombay but, unfortunately, he did leave it lying around amongst his papers. When Napier left India his successor found the report and deliberately brought it into circulation and, as predicted, it was concluded that Burton was an active pederast. Burton claims that this document had the effect of blocking promotions for the rest of his life.

At the end of his years in India Burton returned to England, severely ill. Some biographies mention a return to Oxford in 1850 regarding which he wrote: 'Like the prodigal son I returned to my Alma Mater with a half-resolution to finish my terms and to take my bachelor degree. But the idea came too late. I had given myself up to Oriental studies, and I had begun to write books.' And so his writing had begun in earnest and was to continue in some form or another for the remainder of his life.

The next four years were spent writing books – and in the respectable pursuit of women. He proposed to a few ladies, including his beautiful cousin Elizabeth Stisted to whom he dedicated his first book. Unfortunately for him it appears that his prospects were considered paltry by the families who controlled the lives of the young ladies to whom he paid suit: love was secondary to financial status in those days. However, it was during this time that he met a young lady called Isabel Arundell. It is unlikely that she registered so much as a blip on his radar, but he certainly did on hers. She determined that he was the man for her in every respect except religion. Blessed with a daunting combination of determination and infinite patience she got her man in the end, but it did take a considerable amount of time.

Ever a man of action, Burton acquired the backing of the National Geographic Society for a journey in 1853 to Mecca and Medina. He decided to visit the two secret cities in disguise; non-Muslims were banned on pain of execution. The disguise, according to biographers, even extended to his sexual anatomy: he was circumcised for the trip! At first he decided to use the Persian guise he had adopted to good effect in India, but after arriving in Egypt he learnt that Persians were unwelcome in Mecca and so transformed himself into a Pathan, an Indian of Afghan parentage.

The journey to Mecca via Medina was dangerous and eventful. His caravan was attacked on two occasions and he could barely walk, having stepped on the quill of a sea urchin. But he did reach Mecca and the audacity of the venture and his detailed records of the journey made Burton world-famous: he was widely admired – at least in non-Muslim countries. Strangely, instead of capitalising on his fame by returning to London, Burton travelled from Cairo to Bombay still wearing his flowing robes on board ship. He took two things with him as he left Arabia: detailed notes which he made into a book entitled *Pilgrimage to Al-Medinah and Meccah (1855),* and syphilis which left him with a hatred for Egyptian women.

Other adventures followed. Burton was the first European to enter Harar, the religious capital of Somaliland. As always he found plenty to interest him in the ways of the Somali people and they seemed to really appreciate him – some of the tribesmen accepting him into the tribe and some even offering him wives. It is from these experiences that he began to write about female circumcision and the more unusual disfigurement of infibulation – the sewing together of the vaginal labia to prevent loss of virginity or disloyalty.

Following his visit to Harar, Burton raised an expeditionary force to explore inner Somaliland and to look for the source of the White Nile. John Hanning Speke and two other officers from the Indian Army joined him in Berbera together with forty-two local auxiliaries. But before they could set out they were attacked in the night by a large group of Somalis who suspected that they were spies intent upon destroying the slave trade. The auxiliaries fled, leaving the four Englishmen to defend themselves as best they could. One of them was separated from the group and later found dead. The others defended themselves before escaping to the coast with serious injuries. Burton had a spear thrust through his left cheek, which passed through his palate taking out four back teeth before coming through the other cheek. Not surprisingly given the horrific wound, the scars were with him for the rest of his life. Some said that the scarring added a grimness to his already intimidating appearance.

After a period in the Crimea, where once again he did not see active service, Burton was adopted by Lord Houghton (Monkton Mowles) and through him met many people of power. As an insight into some of the characters in this group we might consider Fred Hankey, a man described as the spiritual ancestor of the modern 'snuff' movie. Hankey rented rooms with a view of the gallows and 'disported with courtesans' whilst watching the hangings take place. Burton visited him in Paris, and though we do not know what took place we have here another indication of the explorer's interest in deviancy.

His next great journey, another attempt to find the source of the White Nile, is widely known. Once again he was accompanied by Speke. The journey was incredibly tortuous. Dogged by fever, it seemed that both men were carried by the natives for much of the time; Burton was unable to walk for eleven of the twenty-one months of the expedition! They did reach their goal, Lake Tanganyika, but could not be sure that it was the source of the Nile. On the return journey Burton stayed in Kazeh to recover from his illnesses whilst Speke set off for another lake that local residents spoke of, an even bigger one to the North. He found the lake (which he named Victoria) and returned elated, certain that he had found the true source of the Nile. Burton was not convinced, though he did admit the possibility. And so began the great controversy that was to lead to Speke's death, killed by his own hand on the day that he and Burton were to debate the whole business of the source of the Nile. In the event Speke was correct: Lake Victoria proved to be the main source, while Lake Tanganyika was shown to be the source of the Congo.

In some senses Burton was at his peak as an explorer at this point: nothing that he did later in life would match that incredible trek to Lake Tanganyika and back. It is a pity that his achievement was sullied by the dispute with Speke, but such problems tended to characterise his life.

His travels continued. He visited America and showed particular interest in the Mormons and their practice of polygamy, yet on his return he married the woman who had pursued him for so long, Isabel. At this point in his life he commenced a new career, earning an income through a string of second-rate Foreign Office appointments. He was consul of Fernando Po in Africa, Santos in Brazil, Damascus in Syria, and finally Trieste, now part of Italy, where he died in post in 1890. Thirty years as a civil servant was hardly a fitting end to a man who showed so much verve, courage and sheer audaciousness. But all was not as it seemed.

It is clear from his writings, and that of many others, that Burton used the consular service to continue his exploration of the world – albeit on a different scale. Throughout the thirty years the consulates served merely as bases from which he could make sorties into the surrounding hinterland. His anthropological studies continued apace and so did his output as a travel writer. And as always there was an air of controversy and jealous dispute.

The final posting was pretty much a sinecure leaving him free to travel and concentrate on his writing. In 1883 Burton suffered a serious heart attack, and the enforced convalescence may have helped him concentrate on translating the ten volumes of *Arabian Nights* (1885-8). The tales are not his of course – he would have heard some of them sitting by the firesides in the deserts of Arabia. They represent a vast collection of stories assembled over many centuries. Most translations toned them down into little more than children's stories, though the originals were often bawdy and sexually explicit. Burton was determined to tell them as they were – even in the Victorian era. He also included notes which provided details of sexual practices around the world.

The publication was a great success. It made more money than anything else that he did in his life. And the *Arabian Nights* led to a visit to Oxford, a grudging but necessary visit. The

Burtons returned to England for a holiday in 1886 and spent some time residing in London. From there Burton wrote a letter to 'the vice-chancellor and the curators of the Bodleian Library' requesting the loan of the Wortley Montagu manuscripts of the Arabian Nights. No doubt these were required for his *Supplemental Nights* which began to appear in that year. He made it clear that this was not a private loan. He wanted them transferred temporarily to the India Office under the charge of a Dr. R. Rost. But the Bod refused his request, just as it had refused the request of Charles I to borrow books during his residency in Oxford at the time of the Civil War – the Bodleian is, after all, a reading library. So Burton was forced to travel to his old university town once more, causing him to observe that 'The Bodleian is the model of what a reading library should not be, and the contrast of its treasures with their mean and miserable surroundings is a scandal.' However, his problems were resolved by having the required pages photographed – and his description of the old library makes a strange contrast to the beauty of the building as it is now.

Burton translated other sexually explicit books, often with collaborators. One of the most famous is the *Kama Sutra* (1883), an Indian sex manual. Others include the *Perfumed Garden* (1886) from Arabia and the *Ananga Ranga* (1885), also from India. It is amusing to recall that Burton and his co-translator, Foster Fitzgerald Arbuthnot, decided to set up their own publishing company, calling it the Kama Shastra Society of London and Benares. The printing was supposedly taking place in India so the printers could not be pursued for prosecution; however the books actually rolled off presses based in Stoke Newington.

In his final years Burton worked on a new version of the *Perfumed Garden* which he called the *Scented Garden*; it promised to be much more explicit but did not see the light of day. On October 19 1890 Sir Richard Burton, explorer, translator and rogue, died in Trieste with the text of the *Scented Garden* more or less complete. This was the end of a life of daring, debauchery and dissidence. A life in which he denied the existence of God, often writing bitterly, and sometimes amusingly, of those who followed the church. His wife had always cherished the desire to convert him to her own belief, and this she did posthumously by engaging a priest to administer the last rights to his cooling body! She then arranged to have him buried as a Catholic, much to the anger of his friends. His grave is a tomb in the shape of an Arabic tent in the cemetery of a small church in Mortlake, a suburb of London.

Shortly after his death Isabel received an offer for the publication of the *Scented Garden* valued at six thousand pounds. But, rather than accept the money, she decided to burn the manuscript! She felt that now that her husband was with God he would not want it released. She also claimed that he appeared three times in her dreams and each time demanded that she burn the manuscript. She was hotly criticised for the destruction; one reaction which seems appropriate in the circumstances called her a hysterical, illiterate woman with 'the bigotry of Torquemada and the vandalism of a John Knox'. Caustic stuff, but not enough to stop her unforgivable trail of destruction. After writing a long and highly personal hagiography of her husband, she burned all of his diaries and journals!

And so the fiery life of Sir Richard Burton ended in the ashes created by his wife. He used to sleep with a map of Africa behind his bed, and above it an Arabic saying which translates as, 'All things pass.' And so did he – but not without notice. Trinity College's official records include a grudging mention of Burton. Following a long list of worthies from its 450-year history, it makes mention of 'individualists, defying classification, such as Sir Richard Burton, explorer of the Nile'. So, even expelled members can get a mention if they do something spectacular with their lives. It's not a bad epitaph for the man at that: 'an individualist defying classification'.

Rogue Assessment:

| | | | | | | | |
|---|---|---|---|---|---|---|---|
| Charmer | [ ] | Womaniser | [ ] | Drinker | [ ] | Liar | [ ] |
| Entertainer | [ ] | Corrupter | [ ] | Adventurer | [ ] | Creator | [ ] |

Sources:
*Snow upon the Desert* by Frank McLynn. John Murray, 1990
*The Life of Sir Richard Burton* by Thomas Wright. IndyPublish.com, 2002
*The Devil Drives* by Fawn M Brodie, Penguin, 1971
*Of No Country* by Frank McLynn. Scribners, 1990
The Trinity College Website
The Oxford University Website
*A Sketch of the Career of Richard F. Burton* by Alfred Bates Richards et al. Waterlow & Sons Limited, 1886

The Old Bodleian Library

# THE AUTHOR
## Graham Greene
*1904-91*

It is just a few steps along the trail from Trinity to Balliol – and yet the two colleges are so very different in size, age, and architecture. At the time of writing Balliol is the largest of the Oxford colleges with more than 600 students. It is also one of the three oldest, having been founded by John de Balliol back in 1263. In complete contrast to Trinity, its young neighbour, it is enclosed by high walls rising directly from the pavements of Broad Street and Magdalen Street, a daunting barrier to those who do not belong.

The southern range that broods over Broad Street is a little intimidating: a high Victorian gothic façade only slightly relieved by fanciful towers and a pleasing variation in height. It gives a strong impression of impregnability, of conservatism, and of moral rectitude. All of this is in direct contrast to the openness, the greenness and the jollity of Trinity.

Henry Graham Greene, better known simply as Graham Greene, entered Balliol in 1922 to study modern history. He was a distant relative of Robert Louis Stevenson and had been educated at Berkhamsted School where his father was headmaster. The school was run with a rod of iron; Greene's father was fearful of sexual immorality and therefore established a network of spies ensuring that the slightest transgression would quickly reach his ears. Deviation was usually rewarded with expulsion. As a boarder at the school, the young Greene had to learn to play the role of a double agent: spying for his father whilst remaining one of the boys. Perhaps the recurring themes of treachery and betrayal in his writings all stem from his troubled school years.

Suicide became a preoccupation. After experimenting with various substances, he resorted to a combination of aspirin and drowning in the school swimming pool – nothing worked. One day he left the school having written a note to his parents saying that he did not wish to return and was going to end it all. Fortunately he was found by his sister who persuaded him to come home. This desperate behaviour culminated in a spell of therapy at the age of fifteen which seemed to be a turning point. The therapist, Kenneth Richmond, encouraged him to write and introduced him to a circle of literary friends which included the poet Walter de la Mare. Some claim the young Greene fell in love with Richmond's wife, so it is possible that this phase was a turning point of another kind. He claimed that his stay with Richmond was 'one of the happiest periods of his life'.

Balliol College was chosen for Greene because Kenneth Bell, a governor of his father's school, was a fellow there; he became Greene's tutor during his stay at Oxford. As an undergraduate he was pretty well off – his father providing an allowance of £250 per annum courtesy of a rich uncle. Despite this generous stipend he was later to recall that his university years were spent in drunkenness and debt. It seems that the 'black dog' that pursued him through his school days had followed him to Oxford.

Balliol College: main entrance on Broad Street

In order to escape boredom Greene took himself off into the country in the direction of the village of Elsfield for Russian roulette sessions with a loaded revolver belonging to an elder brother. He claims to have spun the chamber on six separate occasions, squeezing the trigger whilst holding the cold muzzle to his ear. Each time the single bullet lodged in the chamber did not detonate, and each time he obtained an 'extraordinary sense of jubilation'. But soon the black dog tracked him down again and so he repeated the experience until chance predicted suicide and the 'sense of jubilation' which he had originally obtained had been dulled by repetition. Though the roulette sessions ceased, later in life he became famous for placing himself in dangerous situations: anything from war zones to uncharted territory.

Less drastically he was a member of a group called the Mantichorean Society which carried out pranks such as stealing street notices that declared 'Dogs must be kept on a Lead'. And during one vacation he and a friend hired a barrel organ then wandered around the countryside dressed as tinkers. In this guise he visited his hometown of Berkhamsted and delighted in the fact that he passed through the place unrecognised.

It was at Oxford that Greene made his first contact with the world of espionage. He volunteered his services to the German Embassy as a writer and obtained an all-expenses paid trip to the Rhine in exchange for writing a propaganda article in the *Oxford Chronicle*. Soon after this he took out membership of the British Communist Party in the hope of visiting Russia. He did not succeed in getting to Moscow, but he did contrive a visit to Paris using his party card.

Seemingly drawn to oddly named clubs, he joined one called the Hysteron-Proteron. Rather than collecting silly street signs, this club specialised in living life backwards. For one day in each term the day started with dinner and ended with breakfast – what fun! And, like Rochester, he claims to have been drunk for long periods – a whole term in one case!

His favourite pub was the Lamb and Flag in St Giles, and so it should be – it is an excellent pub even today. Go in, buy a drink, have a look at the notices on the walls. You will discover that the profit made from your beer is used by the owners of the pub, St John's College, to fund PhD students. You will also find an extract from Graham Greene's autobiography in which he writes, characteristically, of the adorable barmaid who then served at the Lamb and Flag. The students christened her Queen Nefertiti and surreptitiously worshipped at her feet, all hoping for an opportunity to walk out with this beauty. But they were to be disappointed: she was captivated by a pipe-smoking don! By the way if you want to see the original Nefertiti (the name meaning 'the most beautiful woman has come'), you can. The Ashmolean Museum in Beaumont Street, almost opposite a house which later was to become the Greene family home, has a fine relief of this Egyptian lady worshipping Aten, the sun god.

During his stay at Balliol, Greene was active on many fronts. He organised a programme for the newly formed BBC radio, assembling a group of six poets, including himself, to give recitals. He also published a book of poetry called *Babbling April* (1925), which attracted little interest. He even finished his first novel, though this did not find a publisher. Perhaps in reaction to this lack of success he became editor of the student magazine, the *Oxford Outlook*, rather famously offering in one of its editions free insurance to its student readership against failure in their exams. 'They had only to fill in the coupon on page 37 and in case of failure they would receive a champagne dinner for two at one of the Oxford restaurants,' he recalls in his autobiography.

Blackwell's Bookshop

It was through his editorship of the magazine that Greene met his future wife, Vivien Dayrell-Browning. He wrote an article putting forward his opinion that there was too much interest in sex in the world and too little in art and religion. Quite an ironic subject given the appetite that he developed for sex in later life. Vivien read the article and sent a note correcting him on a point of Catholic principle (something to do with veneration rather than adoration of the Virgin). Through this he invited her to tea at Balliol where they found they had much in common, including poetry – they had each written collections: Greene's *Babbling April* and Vivien's *The Little Wings* (1918), both published by Blackwell. And it was at Blackwell's bookshop that Vivien worked as an intern.

They quickly became an item – platonic of course, or at least asexual. At one stage Greene proposed converting to the Catholic faith (Vivien was already a convert) and suggested a celibate marriage in order to win the hand of this serious young girl. They were engaged in 1925, the same year in which he obtained his second class honours degree. The engagement is covered merely by one small part of a sentence in his autobiography – but it was written more than forty-five years after the event and a great deal happened to Greene in those intervening years.

Getting a job proved to be very difficult. After two short-lived appointments he became an unpaid sub-editor at the *Nottingham Journal*. He did not seem to like the city much, and it is said that his perception of Nottingham's seediness manifested itself in the novel *Brighton Rock* (1938) – one of his most famous. Nonetheless, this was the city in which he underwent a spiritual transformation. At Oxford he had been a confirmed atheist, at least until Vivien entered the scene. In Nottingham he took instructions in the Catholic faith under Father George Trollope, an ex-actor, and was received into the church in 1926. Whether the conversion was born of a desire to be a good Catholic or born of a desire to marry Vivien will always be a matter for debate. A revealing comment that he made later could indicate a very personal desire: he said that he needed to find a religion against which to measure his evil.

Greene's attitude to adultery and predilection for prostitutes do not seem to square too well with the behaviour of a convinced Catholic, and a story about him indicates a profound disrespect for the religion. He once went into a church with a screenwriter friend, Guy Elmes, with the intention of shocking the priest. Elmes gave a somewhat mild confession but Greene blurted out, 'Father I've fucked an Alsatian this afternoon, how many Hail Marys?' Of course this could have been sheer bravado – who but the priest knows what is said in a confessional?

Greene was not long in Nottingham. He soon obtained a far more prestigious posting as sub-editor at *The Times* in London. And he did get his girl – he married Vivien in October 1927 and they began life together in a small flat in Chelsea. There is an intriguing tale connected to the marriage. Vivien's mother, a strong character by all accounts, gave her daughter a sealed letter addressed to Greene sometime before the ceremony. Vivien was told to give it to him at the beginning of the honeymoon, which she did. He opened it on the wedding night, read it carefully without expression, then tore it up – Vivien never did find out what it said, and no more did anyone else. The letter supposedly related to sex instruction, but whatever could a 1920s mother-in-law have advised her daughter's new husband about in terms of sex – wouldn't we all like to know? Whatever it was we can be pretty sure that congress did ultimately take place since during the time they were together they produced a daughter, Lucy Caroline, and a son Francis.

In the early stages of his marriage Greene wrote a political novel, *The Episode*, which was rejected by publishers. Undeterred he wrote another. This was accepted for publication and it was a winner, reprinted many times and translated into five languages. So Graham Greene had arrived, he was a published author. However, the success of *The Man Within* (1929) led him to face a difficult decision: should he continue with his steady job at *The Times* or become a self-employed writer? His publishers, Heinemann, made the decision easy. They offered him £650 per year for two years providing that he gave them two more novels. He jumped at the chance. Unfortunately, the novels that he produced were not well-received; so he turned his hand to biography, spending many hours at the Bodleian Library carefully researching the life and times of a certain Lord Rochester. Rogue on rogue. The result was *Lord Rochester's Monkey* which Heinemann would not take the risk of publishing in those sensitive times. He did not try elsewhere and forty years were to pass before it was published – in 1974 – the obscenity laws having by then been weakened by the decade of the sixties.

The links between Rochester and Greene are intriguing. They attended colleges which are near neighbours, and though they were separated in time by over 250 years they almost certainly drank in the same hostelries: the King's Arms and the White Horse both lie between the two colleges that they attended. They also had much in common as libertines, writers, and travellers. And both men had a predilection for whores.

It is not clear precisely when Graham Greene began to sample the favours of London prostitutes, but there is no doubt that he did. One source claims that he compiled a list of forty-seven prostitutes whom he recalled from the 1920s and 1930s. Their nicknames were quite revealing, and here are a few: 'Russian Boots', 'Tall Blonde and Friend', 'Nurserymaid', 'Dentist's Assistant', and 'Black Pants'. A friend, Peter Glenville, once observed: 'His sexual stamina always astonished me because it was endless'. And another friend, Michael Meyer, added: 'I always thought that Graham had a rather schoolboy attitude to sex – never for a moment gay, but fascinated by mild divergences from the norm... I remember him suggesting that we find a brothel where two women could put on a lesbian exhibition.'

The roguish side of Greene's character is evidenced by this unashamed womanising, but he could also be a joker. He once made a telephone call to an acquaintance who was giving a party and pretended to be a chimney sweep with orders for a job at the house at seven the next morning. Apparently this spoiled the party. On another occasion he found the number of a namesake in the phone book, rang him and accused him of being the author of 'those filthy books'. The Graham Greene whom he called protested strongly, saying the books were nothing to do with him, that he was in fact a retired solicitor. Greene would not accept this, insisting that if he were the author he would at least admit to it!!

Without the income from Heinemann things began to get tough financially. In 1931, in order to reduce outgoings, he and Vivien rented a small and basic cottage in Chipping Camden for £1 per week. He was a great walker and now found himself in a perfect environment for it – the Cotswolds. On one occasion he walked from Chipping Camden to Stow-on-the-Wold, and on another to Woodstock. These are serious walks.

Living now on his publisher's advances, Greene had to find a way of supplementing his income so he began a second career as a book reviewer, initially working for *The Spectator*. It is possible that this financially strapped period caused him to take a serious look at the content of his novels; his next book was an escapist tale that was deliberately intended to please the public. *Stamboul Train* (1932) was a great success and is probably the portal to his fame as a popular author. Not only was it a bestseller in the book market, the rights were purchased by 20th Century Fox who released the film version as *Orient Express* (1934) in the USA – the beginning for the author of a long-term involvement in the movie world.

The money began to flow again and the little cottage in Chipping Camden was traded for a modern flat in Oxford costing the significant sum of £150 per year. The flat was in Woodstock Close, bang in the middle of the exclusive suburbs of North Oxford and not so far from the lodgings that Graham rented during his last year at Balliol. His first child was born there.

Book then followed book. A trip to Sweden resulted in *England Made Me* (1935), a novel based on a megalomaniacal Swedish financier, his English lover, and her flawed twin brother. But perhaps Sweden was not sufficiently exciting for him. His next trip was to Liberia with an unlikely travelling companion: his cousin Barbara Greene. Together the cousins trekked some 400 miles through this largely uncharted country. An American map available at the time showed the interior as a large white space marked 'cannibals'. Both were lucky to survive the experience which included glimpses of utter poverty together with corruption, sickness and danger. It seems that Greene survived by drinking case after case of whisky. On his return he wrote his first travel book *Journey Without Maps* (1936), and other travel books were to follow.

In 1935 the Greene family moved away from Oxford to a rented house in Clapham Common, London, where they began to mix with the great and good in the literary world. Here he wrote short stories and serials for the papers. He also continued to review books and extended his critical pen into the world of film, once more for *The Spectator*. This interest in film was a strong one; he became involved in screenwriting despite being sued by 20th Century Fox for his criticism of Shirley Temple (he had crossed the line by implying that she was a 'come on' rather than a sweet little innocent). He wrote adaptations for the cinema as well as original screenplays, the most famous among the latter being *The Third Man*. Though this 1949 film gives script credits to a list of people – Graham Greene, Alexander Korda, Carol Reed and Orson Welles – it is based on Greene's original story.

Greene's tendency to place himself in danger continued throughout his life. In 1938 he travelled to Mexico to witness the religious purges which he described in *The Lawless Roads* (1939). The experience of Catholic persecution led him to write a novel, which is often regarded as his finest: *The Power and the Glory* (1940). It won the Hawthornden Prize as well as condemnation by the Vatican.

By this time Greene had attained a career peak with his ideas having a wide influence: the term 'the third man' was used in many different contexts and the 'whisky priest' of *The Power and the Glory* became a universally recognised figure. Then war was declared. He dispatched his family to relative safety with his mother, but the arrangement did not work for long. Vivien moved back to Oxford where she lived in the lodgings of the president of Trinity College, working as companion to the president's wife and as an unpaid servant.

Vivien found life within Trinity College a strain and moved out in 1944, settling in 15 Beaumont Street. Henry James the author had lived at the same address – a fine Georgian-style terraced house located on the corner of Gloucester Street. An article in the *Oxford Mail* reported that there was a notice on the door saying, 'This is not a hotel, nor is it a bed and breakfast, it is not an office or a ministry.' Clearly there were unwelcome callers.

During the war Greene had commenced a long-term affair in London with a lady called Dorothy

Glover, a short, plump, bespectacled lady some years older than himself. He spent time with her in the week and at weekends visited his family in Oxford. In a strange way the affair saved his life! In 1941, when he was sleeping at Dorothy's house, a stick bomb fell directly onto his own Clapham Common home, effectively destroying it. Fortunately it was empty so no one was hurt. It is thought that the relationship with Dorothy contributed to his book *The End of the Affair* (1951) and it is possible to make some link here with the incident at Clapham Common. However, the main inspiration for this was undoubtedly Catherine Walston (later Lady Walston).

The family house in Beaumont Street

The first contact between Catherine Walston and the Greenes occurred when she asked Vivien to persuade her husband to be her godfather, since it was through his books that she had decided to enter the Catholic faith. Greene accepted the role and Vivien attended the ceremony alone. In September 1946 he sent a telegram to his goddaughter saying: 'I feel I am a most neglectful godfather.' At this time they had not met but that Christmas the Greenes were invited to the Cambridge home of Catherine's husband, Labour MP Harry Walston. Catherine flew them back to Oxford in her private plane, her hair blowing wildly across Greene's face (something that he was to recall again and again). He met her once more a few months later in London and fell in love 'over a plate of onions'.

The affair with Catherine Walston was serious, comparable to Richard Burton's 'El Scandale' with Elizabeth Taylor. But whereas 'El Scandale' ended in divorce this affair left everyone unhappily married. Nonetheless there were periods of intense happiness for the author and this is just what he wanted from life: those moments of quintessential emotion that blow the mind. Their affair became public knowledge, especially after publication of *The End of the Affair* (which was dedicated to 'C') and the popular film version released in 1955. For his part Greene was obsessed and tried many times to persuade her to leave her husband.

Public interest in the affair was reawakened by an Oscar-winning remake of the film in 1999, followed by William Cash's book *The Third Woman: The Secret Passion That Inspired The End Of The Affair* which was published at the turn of the century. Clever title, but the book has been subjected to excoriating criticism in the UK. Here is Ian Hamilton of the *Sunday Telegraph* giving his summary of the affair before he rips into Cash's book:

> Both Greene and Walston were married to other people when they met. Greene indeed had a wife, a long-serving mistress and a prostitute-friend who liked him well enough to call him up at home from time to time. Walston, for her part, was a diligent seducer and had a small troupe of admirers at her beck and call. During her time with Greene – which lasted, at full pitch, for something like four years – she was also

around 1600 together with his beautiful and clever wife, Jane. The building is now a shop with offices above; it ceased to be a tavern in 1750. (Incidentally, the tavern is often confused with the Crown Inn which was almost opposite. A part of the inn still exists as a pub operating in a building which was originally the stables: it is hidden away down a little alley formerly known as Draper's Lane.)

The building that was the Crown *Tavern* is of particular interest since it contains a 'painted room'. In 1927 the wooden panelling around this top-storey room was removed to reveal an ancient fireplace and elaborate murals. The latter were dated to the 1500s and hence were there in Davenant's day – they were covered by panelling in 1630. The fireplace is even older, it was part of the original fourteenth-century building.

Site of the Crown Tavern in Cornmarket Street

Why did Shakespeare come to Oxford? In his day the journey from Stratford-on-Avon to the theatres of London was quite an expedition. Some historians say that the roads were so bad in those days that it was quicker to travel by water, taking a boat from Oxford along the Thames. Public stagecoaches, which would have speeded the journey, were not introduced on the Oxford to London route until the reign of Charles II and even then took two days of travelling. For Shakespeare the journey would have taken a minimum of three days with a stay of at least one night in Oxford. At first he stayed at the Crown Inn – some of his papers, now in the British Museum, were found there. But later he became a good friend of John Davenant and so began to stay in the tavern on the other side of Cornmarket.

William Davenant was born at the tavern in 1606, and on March 3 the family strolled over to the nearby St Martin's Church for the christening. Though there seems little doubt that Shakespeare stood as godfather, there is an altogether more shocking and certainly more speculative charge – that he was the boy's biological father. The evidence for this is tenuous and rests mainly on quotations from writers of the day. A chronicler of Oxford, Thomas Hearne, mentions a local tradition that 'Mr Shakespear was his father and gave him his name.' Also from Thomas Hearne comes the story of a young William Davenant running home through the streets of Oxford. He is stopped and asked why he is in such a hurry and replies that his godfather, Shakespeare, has come to stay. He is then told not to take the name of god in vain!

Davenant once wrote a missive to Rochester (presumably the first Earl and John Wilmot's father) containing the following sentence, 'Know this, which does honour to my mother, – I am the son of Shakespeare.' This seems pretty definitive; however, there is a difference between knowledge and belief. A mother usually knows the paternity of her children, whereas the father and child must rely on belief. Furthermore, it is not at all clear why his mother's adultery might do her honour – rather the opposite I think. Perhaps Davenant was simply praising his mother's good taste in mating with the famous playwright. And maybe he was blowing his own trumpet by boasting a blood relationship with the bard.

In the late seventeenth century John Aubrey in *Brief Lives* wrote of Davenant that 'Sir William would sometimes, when he was pleasant over a glass of wine with his most intimate friends, e.g. Sam Butler (author of *Hudibras*), etc – say, that it seemed to him that he wrote with the very spirit that Shakespeare [wrote], and seemed contented enough to be thought his son: he would tell them the story as above, in which way his mother had very light report.'

I suppose we will never know whether William Davenant was truly the biological son of William Shakespeare. And even if he were, then this alone does not qualify him as a rogue, since clearly roguedom is earned not inherited. However, there were events in his later life that certainly qualify him for the title.

In 1621 his father, John Davenant, became Mayor of Oxford but died just six months into his term of office. He was followed to the grave just eighteen days later by his wife. He left behind a very detailed will in which he instructed that the tavern should be kept open for the better relief of his children, and that his two youngest daughters should 'keep the bar by turns' under the supervision of Thomas Hallam, the senior apprentice. Moreover, the will goes on to suggest that Hallam might marry one of his daughters 'if he and she can fancy one another'. He did not specify any role for his son William, merely indicating that he should be 'put to prentice to some good merchant or other tradesman'. There was also a bequest to his son of £150, which probably did not last long; the young Davenant passed much of his life in debt.

In the event William's apprenticeship was not realised. Unlike his brothers who were sent to school in London, he attended the grammar school of All Saints and then entered Lincoln College. This is one of the nearest colleges to the Crown Tavern. Already well-established in Davenant's day, it was founded in 1427 by the bishop of Lincoln and now owns the whole of the southern section of Turl Street, sharing the remainder with Jesus and Exeter. Little is known of his stay there; however, there is a memento of sorts. Above the fire place in one of the smaller meeting rooms hangs a fine portrait of him. Artist and date are not known, in fact the college archivist is not absolutely certain that it is Davenant. But I am. The usual portrait has him with a rotten nose; this portrait is earlier, before syphilis had done its damage. Yet he has the same long prominent chin which, nose aside, is almost his hallmark.

Davenant did not stay the course at Lincoln, choosing instead the life of a royal servant. In 1622 he went to London to become a page to the first Duchess of Richmond and later moved to the household of Sir Fulke Greville, also known as Lord Brooke, a courtier and poet. At the age of eighteen he married a lady called Mary, of whom little is known beyond her name. This was the first of three marriages during his life. He remained in Brooke's household until 1628 when the lord was murdered by an aggrieved servant who discovered that he had not been included in his master's will! Thrown onto his own devices, Davenant took to the stage – writing and directing plays. His first effort, a tragedy called *Albovine*, was produced in 1629 and was followed by another, *The Cruel Brother,* in the following year. And so his new career began – following in his putative father's footsteps.

Lincoln College from Turl Street

It was around this time that he lost his nose, not all of it, but most of it. In one of the few portraits of him that exist this diminutive snout, together with an all-encompassing curly wig, gives the overall appearance of an aristocratic Pekinese dog. His friend, the courtier John Suckling, described the problem of the nose as 'a foolish mischance that he got lately while travelling in France', a clear reference to the 'French Disease' or syphilis. John Aubrey is more direct, and more specific as to origins: 'He gott a terrible clap off a Black handsome wench that lay in Axe-yard, which cost him his nose, with which unlucky mischance many witts were too cruelly bold.' It was an unlucky mischance that he held in common with the 2nd Earl of Rochester.

By 1631 Davenant had recovered sufficiently from the initial phase of the disease to be seen in public, though he claimed he would never again be 'valiant in a strange bed'. Nonetheless, or 'noseless' as it were, his successes continued. In 1634 *The Temple of Love* was performed by the queen and her ladies at Whitehall, after which he appears to have become the queen's favourite poet. Possibly his most famous play, a comedy called *The Wits*, was performed in 1636. Samuel Pepys, the great seventeenth-century diarist, went to see it three times, commenting that it was a 'most excellent play' and on the third viewing professing himself 'most highly pleased'.

In 1637 Davenant produced a masque called *Britannica Triumphans,* but this was banned because its first performance was given on a Sunday. The Puritans were at work. However, things were going well for him at court because, in this same year of 1637, he was made Poet Laureate on the death of Ben Jonson; and in 1639 he became the first manager of the new theatre in Drury Lane. Unfortunately the Civil War was brewing and his flourishing career as playwright and theatre manager was put on hold – the Puritans at work again. And this just at the time that he had been granted a royal patent to build yet another new theatre.

The Civil War (1642-49) was an eventful period for both Davenant and Oxford. Charles I's disputes with his parliament came to a head at the battle of Edgehill after which the king, finding London in control of the Parliamentarians, brought his Royalists to Oxford. And so the city became the Royalist capital for some four years during which the population trebled as the king, his courtiers, the ladies, the servants and the soldiers arrived. As often the city was roughly split in its loyalties between town and gown: the townsfolk favouring the Parliamentary cause, the university and colleges the Royalist.

The colleges were used for all manner of military purposes including arsenals, granaries, powder magazines, cattle pens, and cannon foundries. The king took up residence at Christ Church and held court there. Money was constantly needed to fuel the Royalist cause and so a royal mint was established in New Inn Hall Street – the plate from the colleges being used to create coinage. The walls of the city were repaired and fortified and the city's cornmarket demolished to provide lead for bullets and wood for military engines.

But all this was in vain. Soon after the battle of Naseby the king returned to Oxford recognising that he had 'neither force enough to resist nor sufficient to escape to any secure place'. Ultimately he slipped out of Oxford disguised as a servant in 1646, and later that year the Royalist army surrendered the city to General Fairfax. Oxford's Civil War was at an end but the reparations demanded from the university had just begun, culminating in 1650 when Oliver Cromwell, the Protector, became the chancellor.

Davenant led a dangerous life during this period. An ardent Royalist (though 'town' by birth), he was accused before the Long Parliament of involvement in a bungled army plot to overthrow the House of Commons and was imprisoned for two months. He escaped but was apprehended at Canterbury, escaped again and this time reached the queen in France, remaining there until he volunteered to become a gun-runner for the Royalists. As rogues sometimes do, he rose to the moment and showed so much bravery that, after the siege of Gloucester in 1643, he was knighted by the king. He rejoined the exiles in Paris, where he converted to the Catholic faith and continued his writing.

After the execution of Charles I in 1649, Queen Henrietta dispatched Davenant to America to support the Royalist cause as lieutenant governor of Maryland. But he didn't make it. He had cooked up a scheme to take a number of weavers with him and obtained the permission of the king of France to enter the prisons there to select volunteers. Once the prisoners realised what was on offer, they all cried out that they were weavers – anything to get out of jail. Though he took thirty-six of them with him, he did not get far. His ship was captured in the English Channel by the parliamentarians and he was once again imprisoned in the Tower of London. (What happened to the 'weavers' is not known.)

Davenant's release in 1654 is thought by some to result from the intercession of John Milton. However, in *Brief Lives* John Aubrey claims that it was actually the intervention of a certain Harry Martyn in the House of Commons which saved him. Apparently the House was discussing the execution of one of the Royalist prisoners as an example and Davenant's name was mentioned. Martyn spoke up saying, 'In sacrifices they always offer pure without blemish; now you make talk of sacrificing an old rotten rascal'! Fancy calling one of the Oxford rogues an 'old rotten rascal'!

What happened to Mary, Davenant's first wife, is not at all clear. They had two children. One, a son, died in 1651 at the Crown Tavern in Oxford. The second, a girl, married an uncle of Jonathan Swift. Swift obtained his MA from Hertford College and the uncle was a fellow at Balliol. It is assumed that Davenant's daughter met her husband whilst staying at the Crown Tavern which was then run by Davenant's sister, Jane.

Soon after leaving the Tower Davenant married again, this time to a lady called Ann Cademans. She was the rich widow of the doctor who had nursed Davenant through that attack of syphilis which destroyed his nose. However, her fortune clearly did not last long since her husband was soon arrested for debt (Davenant's tailor had him arrested four times on this charge). He applied directly to Oliver Cromwell for release based mainly on the fact that he had already served two years in the Tower. It worked and he was discharged.

Soon after this Ann Cademans died and Davenant inherited her four sons. He quickly married again, this time to a French lady, Henrietta-Maria du Tremblay, whom he had met whilst an exile in France. This was a most successful marriage with many male offspring and a partnership that extended into William's later career.

Cromwell and his followers were no lovers of the stage – they banned theatre during the Commonwealth. Yet somehow Davenant managed to extract permission in 1656 to produce an opera (as distinct from a play); the trick was that the ban covered drama but not music. It was staged in a private room in his home, Rutland House, in London in order to avoid the severe censorship laws that existed in those puritanical days. Entitled The *Siege of Rhodes*, it is claimed to be the first public opera performed in England, also the first to have painted stage sets and a female singer. According to John Aubrey the performance was very good: 'It did affect the ear and the eye extremely.'

In 1659 Davenant showed his lasting Royalist allegiance by taking part in Sir George Booth's insurrection in Cheshire. This was one of many that were planned in that year, though the only one to come to fruition. The insurgents did take Chester, but were soon soundly beaten by the Parliamentarian army. Davenant was imprisoned once more, and, on his release, returned to France. With his loyal record he was very much in favour with Charles II when the Commonwealth ended in 1660 and the restored monarch took the throne.

Together with Thomas Killigrew (the man whose ears were boxed by Lord Rochester), Davenant was given a royal patent to form a theatre company. Cromwell the Puritan was dead, long live the stage! He founded the Duke of York's Playhouse in Lincoln's Inn Fields, later transferring his charter to Covent Garden where, together with the poet John Dryden, he wrote an adaptation of Shakespeare's *The Tempest* which was performed in 1667.

Davenant was to have a special role, some say a pivotal role, in the popularisation of Shakespeare's plays. Alfred Harbage in his 1935 biography claims that he is 'the chief conduit through which Shakespearean stage tradition has reached us today'. One of his major contributions was a freshening up of the plays by adapting them to the current political climate, something that has continued to the present and is said to account for Shakespeare's enduring popularity. Meanwhile, Davenant's own plays are virtually unknown nowadays – rather than being son to a famous father he was, perhaps, the founder of his father's fame.

After a varied life as a poet, playwright, theatre manager, gun runner, rogue and loyal royalist, he died at his house in Lincoln's Inn Fields on April 7, 1668. He is buried in Poets' Corner, Westminster Abbey. His inscription reads 'O rare Sir William Davenant!' which is certainly a much better epithet than 'old rotten rascal'.

Rogue Assessment:

| | | | | | | | |
|---|---|---|---|---|---|---|---|
| Charmer | [ ] | Womaniser | [ ] | Drinker | [ ] | Liar | [ ] |
| Entertainer | [ ] | Corrupter | [ ] | Adventurer | [ ] | Creator | [ ] |

Sources:

*Encyclopaedia Britannica*, Eleventh Edition, Volume VII. Anonymous. Cambridge University Press, 1910. p. 851-2.
*William Shakespeare* by Victor Hugo. Chicago: A.C. McClurg and Co, 1886
*An Encyclopaedia of Oxford Pubs, Inns and Taverns* by Derek Honey. Oakwood Press, 1998
'Sir William Davenant'. Wikipedia, 2008
*Sir William Davenant, Poet Venturer* by Alfred Harbage. Oxford University Press, 1935
*Aubrey's Brief Lives*, edited by Oliver Lawson-Dick. Mandarin, 1992
*Rare Sir William Davenant* by Mary Edmond. Manchester University Press, 1987
*The Encyclopaedia of Oxford* edited by Christopher Hibbert. Macmillan, 1988

The Mitre on the High Street

# THE MEDIA MOGUL
## Robert Maxwell
*1923-91*

The trail now leaves Cornmarket, turning into Market Street where the back entrances of the Covered Market face the high walls of Jesus College. At Turl Street we turn to the right and are now in Lincoln College territory. The college is on the left and it is usually possible to peek into its gorgeous fifteenth-century front quad, the walls laced with creeper and the grass so green it seems to glow. It probably looked much the same in Davenant's day. The house beyond is that of the head of Lincoln – the rector

The Mitre pub is on the western corner of the junction of Turl Street and the High and on the other corner is All Saints Church. The pub, the oldest in Oxford, was given to the church in the fourteenth century as a chantry, and the church was given to Lincoln College by its founder – the Bishop of Lincoln. So now Lincoln owns the lot, using the church as its library and the upper stories of the pub as student accommodation. Along the High, beyond All Saints, is Brasenose (the only college named after its own doorknocker). This range of the college was designed by the excellent Victorian architect T.G. Jackson in a style which is sometimes called Jacobethan – a subtle merging of the Jacobean and Elizabethan styles. It boasts one of Oxford's most famous grotesques (meaning: a dry gargoyle), the one that unconcernedly picks its nose whilst looking impassively over the traffic surging along the street below.

St Mary's Church follows the delightful curve of the High as it slopes off to the east. The church existed at the time of the Domesday Book, though it is much changed since the eleventh century. It acted then as the main centre of learning and it is still the university church to this day; Oriel College, opposite, appoints the vicar. In the early fourteenth century the church was enlarged, both widthways and upwards. An extension was added alongside the chancel to provide a meeting room for the university's convocation, then the most important management body, and above this the university's first library was added. The ground floor of this extension now forms a pleasant café.

The impressive spire, also built in the fourteenth century, now aligns with the café rather than the altar – an unusual arrangement for a church. You can climb a narrow spiral staircase to an observation walkway at the base of the spire, which provides one of the best views of Oxford. It offers a panorama that explains why a past professor of poetry, Matthew Arnold, penned the famous line describing Oxford as 'the city of dreaming spires'. And so it is.

St Mary's Church tower

The first of the viewing balconies looks north over the stunning Radcliffe Square – Oxford's architectural centre of gravity. The southern balcony looks directly onto the High Street frontage of Oriel College, providing a good view of the statue of the man who paid for it: Cecil Rhodes, founder of the Rhodes Scholarships. The eastern balcony looks down towards Magdalen College and is of particular interest here since one's eye is taken by the gentle slope of South Park as it rises towards Headington. Look to the left, high up and almost in a line with the copper-green cupola of the bell tower of Queen's College, and you can see a large mansion rising through an abundance of trees. This is Headington Hill Hall, now a part of Brookes University but previously the home of Robert Maxwell: our next rogue.

Maxwell is described in *Brewer's Rogues, Villains and Eccentrics* (2004) as a politician, publisher and embezzler! *Private Eye* called him the 'Bouncing Czech'. Others knew him as 'Captain Bob' or, within his business empire, as 'RM'. He was a big man and a bully. He is perhaps the least likable of our rogues – yet some people loved him.

Maxwell's origins are a little obscure. He was born of Jewish parents in 1923 in a town that has had various names: Szlatina, Akanazlatina and Solotvino. This same town has, at one time or another, belonged to Hungary, Czechoslovakia, and Poland; and, when part of the Soviet Union, was within Ukraine. Perhaps this strange springboard helped to shape the young boy.

During his early years he changed names as frequently as most of us change addresses. Born as Lev Hoch, he became Jan Ludvik Hoch when his town became part of Czechoslovakia. At the onset of war he made an epic journey from Hungary through Yugoslavia and on to Western Europe with a group of Czech volunteers. On reaching England he adopted the name Ivan Du Maurier, after the famous cigarette brand, and enrolled in the infantry. He later sought anonymity under the name Leslie Smith and then Leslie Jones before finally alighting on Ian Robert Maxwell, probably after the famous brand of coffee.

At war he did enough brave things to rise through the ranks to become Captain Maxwell and receive the Military Cross. In one courageous attack he was the only person to survive from the unit that he led. An accusation that Maxwell had shot unarmed civilians during the war led to this rebuttal by Ronald Dale of Witney near Oxford who fought alongside him in Holland and Germany in the Queen's Royal Regiment: 'I was in Maxwell's platoon and I was with him nearly every day – I think we would have known about it.' He also added, 'He was a good shot and he was the bravest man I have ever met. He was a credit to the British Army.'

At the war's end he became an interrogator of Nazis in Holland and afterwards a newspaper censor in Berlin. He was the sort of man who always had petrol where most had none; the sort of man who equipped his men with watches confiscated from German captives so that meetings could be held on time. He spoke excellent English and claimed to have mastered nine separate languages during his life – almost a Sir Richard Burton in the making. A close colleague claims that he carried a copy of Machiavelli's *The Prince* (1532) with him at all times.

The cocktail of information gatherer, sharp commercial operator and linguist undoubtedly helped to create an ideal skill base for his future career. He began to specialise in the publication of scientific information and found a supporter in MI6: the British intelligence unit funded his start-up cost to the tune of £30,000 – an investment targeted primarily at the extraction of information from the Soviet Union. His initial success was also aided by another role in postwar Berlin – he was in charge of paper for printing and this brought him into contact with academic publishers as they struggled to re-establish their businesses.

He formed a UK company to distribute the publications of Springer, a German company, which is still today a publisher of scientific journals and books. Springer was heavily constrained by postwar regulations so Maxwell's company helped to re-establish its trade links with the rest of Europe. This co-operative venture was to form the underlying platform of his future commercial activities – the purveying of scientific knowledge. His original company went through several mergers and machinations to emerge as Pergamon Press which expanded beyond the distribution of Springer's publications to publishing its own journals and books. And so his empire grew, through aggressive take-overs, mergers, and flotations – utilising all of the machinations of corporate gerrymandering.

By 1953 Maxwell was a very rich man, with offices and a penthouse flat in London. Travelling the country in his chauffeur-driven Rolls Royce, he came to Oxford where he purchased the lease of Headington Hill Hall and its grounds from the local council for a peppercorn rent of £2,400 per year. The hall had been built in 1824 by the Morrell family, local brewers, and with it came thirty-seven acres of parkland. It lies just to the east of central Oxford and has an excellent view of the 'dreaming spires' across the valley of the River Cherwell. A well-proportioned mansion surrounded by trees and grassy slopes, for many years it served as the Maxwell family home as well as the Pergamon headquarters.

And so Robert Maxwell became Britain's richest council house tenant, constructing a large office block in the grounds of the hall together with many unsightly prefabricated buildings. Today the hall contains at least one memory of its previous tenant. The fine entrance lobby has an impressive staircase leading to a strange stained-glass window – this window was designed by an Israeli artist and depicts Maxwell himself as Samson! It replaces a Victorian study of Samson at the gates of Gaza which was damaged during the war.

There are many stories about this large, and larger-than-life, man, ranging from his gluttony to his generosity; from his abrupt, unfeeling treatment of his staff to his careful use of insinuation to gain access to the lives of world leaders. These stories help to shed light on the man who ran the 'Purgatory Press' as some called it. Here are a couple of my favourites which I have second-hand from a fellow Oxford guide, Ted East, who knew Maxwell's driver well.

The first is a double-edged story set in the Pergamon Press building. One day Maxwell was striding along one of the corridors and saw a man approaching from the other direction. The man was smoking a cigarette and, though Maxwell liked a cigar himself, he could not tolerate people smoking in his buildings. He stopped the man and thundered:
'Tell me. Just how much do you earn in a year?'
The man looked baffled, but replied, 'About twelve hundred pounds.'

At this Maxwell took out his wallet, counted twelve hundred pounds (he always carried plenty of cash) and bellowed: 'Take that. You're fired. Leave the building and take your cigarettes with you.' The man shook his head in perplexity, took the money and walked off. It turned out later that he was, in fact, a local telephone engineer who had been called in to fix a fault. He did not work for Maxwell at all!

Ted East also told me another interesting story about the problems of working for Maxwell. Ted had been a senior policeman, and when retirement came he and a colleague both applied for the post of marshal at Oxford University. The other man got the job, but turned it down because he did not want to live in the grace-and-favour house in central Oxford that came with it. So Ted became marshal while the other man took a better-paid job as Maxwell's driver. On one occasion Ted met his old friend's wife. He asked her how her husband was doing.
'Not so good,' she said with obvious concern. 'Do you think that you could get him a job in the university?'
'Why's that?' asked Ted, puzzled.
'That man Maxwell is killing him,' she replied then, pausing briefly, she continued, 'With work.'

It seems that Maxwell would call his driver at any time of day or night and expect him to drop everything in order to take him somewhere. On one occasion Maxwell decided, on the spur of the moment, that he had to go to New York. He called the driver at two in the morning and off they went. Maxwell had no ticket and when they got to the airport all of the flights were fully booked. Unperturbed, he gave an impromptu speech saying that he just had to see his aging mother who was sick and dying in New York. Some sympathetic passenger actually believed the story, gave up their ticket, and off Maxwell flew!

That his behaviour verged on megalomania is beyond question. He was known to have himself paged at airports simply to let everyone know he was there! Also, many a headwaiter at a fully booked restaurant would find Maxwell at his shoulder pointing to 'his booking' – a booking which was for whichever name was next up for a table! He recruited a number of ex-policemen in Oxford who had left the force for dubious reasons – his assistant called them 'the thugs'.

They hung out in the gatehouse building of Headington Hill Hall and accompanied Maxwell to union meetings etc, protecting him from angry crowds. One of them travelled everywhere with him, both at home and abroad, ostensibly as his cameraman. They were part of the 'inner circle': loyal, long-term servants and assistants who were paid well and who were expected in return to give all to their boss.

Maxwell's council house: Headington Hill Hall.

Maxwell's desire for power was ill-concealed: perhaps he did not care to conceal it. As indicated by the smoking story, he sought to wield unconstrained power within his companies. And he wanted yet more. In 1964 he was elected the Labour MP for Buckingham, but once in the House of Commons he showed himself far too ambitious for a new boy – far too forward. He was also tainted by his rapacious capitalism, which would never do for the left wing of the Labour party. He had entered the Commons looking upward, maybe to a spell at 10 Downing Street, but the only position he achieved during his years in parliament (which ended in 1970) was chairman of the House of Commons Catering Club committee. Not quite what he had in mind I'm sure, but then he did like his food. It was during Maxwell's watch that the valuable wine cellars were raided to create cash needed to balance the books which, until then, had languished in the red!

With little prospect of political power at home, he began a campaign to win the hearts and minds of foreign heads of state, particularly through the *Leaders of the World* publications by Pergamon. As series editor Maxwell had a close hand in these hagiographies and, consequently, a direct line to overseas leaders – particularly those of the communist regimes of Eastern Europe and the Soviet Union. There are still rumours that this loss-making series was a cover for spying activities (for the KGB, or MI6, or both), but this is unlikely. His game plan appears to have been more grandiose.

Through his dealing with the Soviet Union, and Brezhnev in particular, Maxwell was able to predict the collapse of communism. In fact he made this point in a speech to the House of Commons as early as 1968 when preaching restraint over the crushing of Czechoslovakia's 'Communism with a human face'. His ambition was to be around when the collapse of communism came, ready and willing to pick up the pieces by injecting capitalism (or Maxwellism) and reaping the rewards. Consequently he became close to Todor Zhivkov of Bulgaria, Wojciech Jaruzelski of Poland and, to a lesser extent, Mikhail Gorbachev of the Soviet Union.

Meanwhile, his commercial empire grew and Maxwell grew with it. Then came something new, a take-over approach by an American company called Leasco in the early 1970s. Naturally Leasco wanted to see Maxwell's accounts before the deal was signed, and their examination exposed a great deal of creative accounting. The discovery led to the involvement of the Board of Trade, which conducted a detailed investigation of Pergamon exposing irregularities in the company's accounting practices. The report ended with a damning statement shrouded in grudging praise: 'We regret having to conclude that, notwithstanding Mr Maxwell's acknowledged abilities and energy, he is not in our opinion a person who can be relied on to exercise proper stewardship of a publicly quoted company.' Naturally Maxwell was furious, instigating legal action to get the harsh criticisms rescinded but without success.

Despite the Board of Trade's biting comments, Maxwell recovered and went on to extend his business empire still further until, in 1984, he took over the United Kingdom's Mirror Group Newspapers from Reed International. Many say that the *Mirror* became a pet creature of Maxwell's, such that it featured the mogul's publicity-grabbing activities above other news items. He moved into the penthouse at the top of the Mirror building and, on one occasion, cleaners claim that they found the bones of six chickens on the floor and a toilet that looked as if a horse had used it. This, together with reports of his unzipping his trousers as he emerged from his helicopter on top of the Mirror building and peeing over the balustrade, certainly does not suggest an attractive character. Whilst urinating on those below, he opined that this was what he thought of his readers!

There is little doubt that he was an arrogant man who was determined to get his own way; a man who believed that rules were made for others, not himself. A friend of mine who worked for him told me about an incident that took place during a conference in the college of Christ Church. Normally motor vehicles are not allowed to pass through the gates of Tom Quad, but such rules are for normal mortals. Maxwell simply drove his brown Rolls Royce through the entrance and parked it on the grass of that beautiful quad. He stepped out of the car, ignored everyone, and walked to the hall. Arrogance overcomes all.

He was a big man and, well … fat. After one of his top-level meetings with Gustav Husak of Czechoslovakia, he was invited to take part in a hunting trip in the grounds of the president's summer palace. However, there were two problems: first his host could not find any hunting trousers big enough for Maxwell's huge girth, and secondly there was no horse available to bear his huge weight. He was therefore loaded onto a cart and off he charged into the forest wearing a Czech coat of hunting green over his ordinary business trousers.

Mike Maloney, a photographer permanently assigned to Maxwell, tells an amusing story of an event which took place in the Soviet Union. Maxwell was waiting to see Gorbachev and was in a foul mood. His staff were sitting in uncomfortable wrought-iron chairs around a large table. Maxwell sat in the largest of the chairs, lambasting his staff one by one. He was seething with rage, a rage no doubt fuelled by the barely suppressed sniggering of his staff as they noticed that the great man was slowly sinking. Maxwell was simply too heavy for the wrought-iron legs of his chair, which slowly buckled under his great weight.

Every Friday Maxwell had a regular spot on Radio Oxford, usually conducted by telephone. One announcement in 1986 concerned the libel action against *Private Eye* magazine which he had just won. 'Good evening listeners,' he said. 'No doubt you have heard that I have taken £50,000 off that scurrilous magazine *Private Eye*. I am going to give the money to AIDS research. And I can tell you that I am going to write a book about my experiences and it is to be called *Malice in Wonderland*.'

The book was indeed written – by Maxwell's staff. What's more, a spoof version of *Private Eye* was rolled off the Pergamon printing press. Called *Not Private Eye,* it lampooned the editorial staff of the magazine, copying its style and content. Contributors to the take-off included Clive Jenkins, Ken Livingstone, Spike Milligan, Michael Parkinson and Mary Whitehouse. Nearly a million copies were printed; no one knows how many were sold but revenge was both expensive and sweet for Robert Maxwell – the 'bouncing Czech' had bounced back.

In 1981 Maxwell took over the British Printing Corporation and with it a subsidiary, Sun Printers of Watford. Brian Reynolds was a director of Sun Printers and recalled in an interview with the BBC his impressions of Maxwell: 'I was surprised by his stature, his presence and his impeccable English accent. He used Grecian 2000 and often wore a blue suit with flamboyant ties. We always got on well. His manner towards me was friendly and enquiring. He would remember what you'd said.' But he was also aware of the other side of his new boss: 'Others found him abrasive and were unable to adapt or reconcile themselves to his style. I did see colleagues bullied. Standing up to him seemed to the best way – at least he'd acknowledge this.'

In 1982 Maxwell became the owner and chairman of Oxford United Football Club, saving the club from bankruptcy and pushing the team to heights not seen before or since. In 1984 the club was promoted to division one of the Football League, furthermore, in that same year and in typically Maxwellian style, the chairman attempted to merge the club with Reading to form Thames Valley Royals. The attempt failed. Bouncing back from this failure, Maxwell then bought Derby Football Club and left his son Kevin to look after Oxford.

Buying football teams for the rich is akin to buying racehorses – but the profile is much higher. Popular with the northern club at first, Maxwell lost the backing of the fans when they realised that the promised funds needed to lift the team into the first division were not forthcoming. 'He's fat, he's round, he's never on the ground. Captain Bob, Captain Bob!' they cried when he turned up at the stadium for one of his infrequent visits – straight out of his helicopter.

The helicopter was a regular means of transport for Maxwell. On one occasion he struggled aboard with his leg encased in plaster following a breakage. During the journey he complained that his leg was hot and opened a window to stick his broken limb out into the streaming air. This caused a vortex which sucked all the papers in the helicopter out of the window and onto the fields below; the papers included a huge file on parking problems at the Mirror building. On his return to London he blandly announced to his staff that he had 'solved the parking problem'.

Peter Jay, who had been the UK's ambassador to the United States, became Maxwell's 'Chief of Staff' and travelled extensively with his boss, often in the helicopter. When asked why Maxwell wanted him along on these journeys, he suggested that his boss liked a retinue who would always be at his beck and call. His own particular skill, he recalled, was in the writing department since Maxwell was 'almost entirely unable to put two words together on paper'.

Robert Maxwell left his mark on Oxford in many ways. In a fairly typical demonstration of the 'soft skills' that he applied to industrial disputes he fired twenty-three people from Pergamon because they were union members. They remained 'on strike' at Headington Hill Hall for many years, picketing at the main entrance gate to the estate. A monument to their struggle is set in a flower-bed at the top of Headington Hill, just outside the entrance to the grounds of the hall. It reads:

> At this site, between May 1989 and September 1992, 23 members of the National Union of Journalists mounted a continuous and united picket in defence of union rights at Robert Maxwell's Pergamon Press. His empire collapsed; the union lives on.

Maxwell as Samson in Headington Hill Hall

It is true, the empire did collapse. Over–stretched by loans resulting from the purchase of the *New York Daily News* he began, as one biography has it, to bale water back into the sinking ship. Money from pension funds and the day-to-day operation of his companies was used to buy shares in his two public companies: Maxwell Communications and the Mirror Group. He even sold Pergamon, the company that he had founded back in 1951, to raise money for his purpose. The share-buying was intended to boost the stock of the companies against which his loans were secured. It did not work.

On November 5, 1991, he was reported missing from his luxury yacht off the Canary Islands. Later that day his bloated body was found floating, face up, some twenty miles southwest of Gran Canaria. He died leaving a massive £400m hole in the pension funds of his companies and thereby condemning many of his workers to an impoverished retirement. The Mirror Group pensioners reacted by mounting a massive campaign for compensation and, after some years, most of their funds were recovered thanks to a £100m government contribution plus out-of-court settlements from City institutions. Former employee Brian Reynolds was lucky but did change his opinion of Maxwell: 'My pension had been transferred to another scheme so was safe, but some colleagues did suffer. I'd admired him for being a man who'd never forgotten his background and who generated employment for thousands of people. But now of course, I feel let down. Because he betrayed so many. Still – he's someone I'll never forget.'

In an obituary in the *Independent* newspaper he was described as a 'foulmouthed, arrogant, gluttonous rogue'. Many mysteries surrounding this intriguing man have never been put to rest – perhaps they never will be.

Rogue Assessment:

| | | | | | | | |
|---|---|---|---|---|---|---|---|
| Charmer | [ ] | Womaniser | [ ] | Drinker | [ ] | Liar | [ ] |
| Entertainer | [ ] | Corrupter | [ ] | Adventurer | [ ] | Creator | [ ] |

Sources:
*Foreign Body: The Secret Life of Robert Maxwell* by Russell Davies. Bloomsbury, 1995
*Maxwell Stories* by Sam Jaffa. Robson Books, 1992
*The Unknown Maxwell* by Nicholas Davies. Sidgewick and Jackson, 1992
'Maxwell - the man in the blue suit' Radio Oxford. December 5, 2005
*Headington History* by Stephanie Jenkins. www.headington.org.uk, 2008
'Travels with Cap'n Bob' BBC Radio 4. January 5, 2008

The view from St Mary's Church towards Headington Hill Hall, just visible in the trees

# THE PRESIDENT
## Bill Clinton
*1946-*

Descending the dark and narrow stairway of St Mary's tower we emerge, blinking in the sunlight, onto the High and continue along the trail by crossing the road. There, alongside the eastern boundary of Oriel College, lies Magpie Lane which takes its name from the Magpie Inn, now long gone. It is an interesting pathway which broadens into a road as it heads towards Merton Street. The lane contains some of Oxford's few remaining medieval houses: one wood-framed building is marked with its date of origin – 1588. The original name for the street was Gropecunt Lane, a dark and disreputable place in the thirteenth century and a dalliance for prostitutes.

About halfway down the lane there is a turning to the left into Kybald Street. Ignore the robust modern building on the southern corner, this belongs to Corpus Christi, and look left towards a solid but attractive block of houses set some hundred metres in from Magpie Lane. These were almshouses built for poor men and women in 1816 and funded by an alderman called John Parsons. In 1959 an American couple paid for new almshouses in the St Clements area of Oxford and donated the old ones to University College which uses them as student accommodation. The front doors are sealed off and entrance is from Helen's Court within the college. This is where, in 1968, our next rogue Bill Clinton came to live.

Clinton needs no introduction – he is arguably the most famous of Oxford's non-graduates (he did not complete his course) and the most well-known ex-president of the USA. His childhood reads like a slice of American pie, with a few unfortunate blemishes. He was born in Hope, a small town in the state of Arkansas, to a widowed mother – tragically his father had died in a motorcar accident less than three years into the marriage and three months before the future president was born. His mother re-married, and it is from his binge-drinking, gun-toting stepfather that Clinton takes his surname.

When Bill was seven, the Clintons moved to Hot Springs, his stepfather's hometown, where the young boy thrived at the local school. Playing the saxophone was his favourite pastime; he practised every day and became a top player winning a prize with the state band. He was also a delegate to Boys State, a summer school which introduced young lads to local government (there was a Girls State too), and was elected a delegate to Boys Nation which meant a trip to Washington to gain experience of national government. This 1963 visit was the turning point in his life. In Washington he met, and shook hands with, President John Kennedy just four months before his assassination. And in that same year he warmed to Martin Luther King's 'I have a dream' speech on television, memorising the entire thing. His ambition to become president of the United States dates from this time.

Clinton entered Georgetown University in Washington with the help of scholarships and loans. During this time he worked as an intern for J. William Fulbright, an Arkansas Senator, and gained more experience of the machinations of government. Fulbright became one of his role models. The senator had been a Rhodes scholar and a student at Pembroke College, so maybe this is where Clinton's Oxford connection begins. In 1968, with the shadow of the draft board and service in Vietnam hanging over him, he too applied for a Rhodes Scholarship.

Magpie Lane, off High Street

The scholarships were founded by Cecil Rhodes, an Englishman who made his money primarily from diamond mining in South Africa. Rhodes returned to his home country at the age of nineteen in order to study for a degree. Rejected by University College, he walked up the High to Oriel where he was accepted. The college's reward was considerable – the former student's legacy paid for the entire new frontage of the college on the High which faces the university church. However, the bulk of his legacy was used to fund the Rhodes Scholarships and to construct the imposing Rhodes House in Parks Road. Since 1903 scholarships have been awarded to some 80 students each year, drawn from various Commonwealth countries plus the United States and Germany.

For his application Clinton had to acquire letters of recommendation from eight worthies, write an essay explaining why he wanted to come to Oxford, and convince an interview committee that he possessed the required 'truth, courage, and devotion to duty', together with the 'moral force of character and instincts to lead, and to take an interest in one's fellow beings'. In 1968 he sailed to England along with 31 fellow Rhodes scholars on the SS United States – the trip took nearly one week therefore allowing time, in Clinton's words, for 'sniffing each other out'. What an adventure! It was on this voyage that he claims to have enjoyed his very first 'snifter', starting with Scotch and soda, then progressing to bourbon and water.

At Oxford Clinton slipped quickly into the life of University College (often abbreviated to Univ), settling upon a B.Phil course in politics. In his first year he travelled a lot, read a lot (200 books in one year!) and made many friends, particularly amongst other Rhodes scholars. He did not take his studies too seriously as there were other things on his mind: bicycling, socialising and the Vietnam War. Later he recalled that his first two weeks were mostly spent walking around the city: 'I explored its rivers, parks, tree-lined paths, churches, the covered market, and of course the colleges.' Interestingly he doesn't mention pubs.

Reminiscing about his stay in Oxford at the famous Hay-on-Wye book festival, he recalled a trip by bus to Cardiff with his friend Rick Stearns. 'I had not read poetry before I came to Oxford. The only poem I had read was Dylan Thomas' "Do Not Go Gently into That Dark Night". I liked it a lot because it became the philosophy of my life... I had never been to Thomas' birthplace in west Wales, so I said to a classmate that I'd like to know more about him. We took a bus trip from Oxford to Cardiff. I remember it took forever to get there. We got out at the bus station in Cardiff; we stopped at a little pub, there was a Jerry Lewis film on the television – I remember that. We drank a lot of beer and read these poems to each other and I thought they were fabulous.' They didn't make it to Dylan's birthplace.

In the summer term of his first year, Clinton was called up (drafted as they say in the United States). One of his American colleagues, Frank Aller, had decided to avoid the draft by staying on in England and Clinton supported him since he thought the war unwinnable and believed the USA should not be in Vietnam. However, perhaps with an eye to the future, he himself did not want to be labelled a draft dodger.

At the end of his first year he visited Paris with a young woman called Alice Chamberlain whom he had met in London through mutual friends. He returned to Oxford and, early in the morning, climbed to the rooftop of one of the college buildings to watch the sun coming up over the city skyline with 'English friends'. Later he recalled that, 'we were so pumped up we broke into the Univ kitchen, pinched some bread, sausages, tomatoes, and cheese, went back to my room for breakfast.' So Bill Clinton could be a naughty boy. After the party he returned to the USA, ostensibly to join the armed forces.

But he did not join up. Instead one of his Oxford friends and a fellow Arkansan, Cliff Jackson, helped him to dodge the draft by becoming part of the Reserve Officers Training Corp and enrolling in an Arkansas law school. But he reneged on this deal, making his way back to Oxford as a dodger of a different sort. Conscience-stricken he fought a fierce internal battle between his opposition to the war in Vietnam and his need to show himself a patriotic American. He was saved by President Nixon who, on gaining the presidency, changed the rules by introducing a ballot system for the draft. Clinton then abandoned his dodge and entered the lottery with a clear, well sort of clear, conscience. He drew a high number and thus avoided military service entirely. Funny how things work out sometimes.

Oxford is a city of cyclists, and it was at Oxford that Bill Clinton learned to ride a bike: a proper, two-wheeled bike! As a child he had used trainer wheels and, believing that he had a balance problem, denied himself the freedom of two wheels. But now as an Oxford student he found that he could cycle without help. Maybe it was the effect of the bourbon? Or maybe the dope? Surely it wasn't dope, after all it was of his Oxford days that he famously stated, 'I experimented with marijuana a time or two, and I didn't like it. I didn't inhale and never tried it again.'

Coincidentally there is a link with Howard Marks here. In his second year at Oxford Clinton lived at 46 Leckford Road, the same house from which Howard Marks had been 'abducted' a few years earlier. Later when the drug dealer languished in a federal jail, reporters from the *Mail on Sunday* arrived to interview him, claiming to have incontrovertible evidence that he and Clinton had lived together at Leckford Road. Though this was quite untrue, Marks characteristically did not deny it. In his autobiography he made the pithy comment: 'I never met anyone who smoked joints without inhaling.'

Kybald Street: Clinton's University College rooms

During that second year Bill Clinton travelled more extensively – one trip, taken over the long winter break, lasted for 40 days! He visited Amsterdam, Sweden and Finland, then went on to the Soviet Union returning via Prague and Munich. He met many people, often linking up with fellow Americans. In his book, *Unlimited Access* (1998), former FBI agent Gary Aldrich states that Clinton left Oxford for a 'European Tour' in 1969 and was told by university officials that he was no longer welcome in the institution. Aldrich claimed Clinton's academic record at Oxford was lacklustre.

True or not, Clinton had to make a big decision at the end of the year: to continue his studies for the third year of his B.Phil or return to America and begin studying for a law degree at Yale. He chose the latter and thus left Oxford without a qualification.

Clinton is a good-looking man with an easy smile and clean-cut features that many women find desirable. Naturally, given the revelations concerning his sexual adventures, there has been a media hunt for ex-girlfriends from his Oxford days. He mentions liaisons in his autobiography, stating that he had a problem forming lasting relationships. In fact the woman who seems to have made the greatest impression on him was Mandy Merck, the 'first openly lesbian woman' he had ever known.

A political news site on the web, Capitol Hill Blue (launched in 1994 and claiming to be the oldest of its kind), maintains a long list of women who say that Clinton sexually assaulted them at some point in his life. It begins with Eileen Wellstone, a nineteen-year old English woman who claimed that he assaulted her after she met him at a pub near Oxford. Though Clinton admitted having sex with the girl, he claimed it was consensual and the victim's family declined to pursue the case. In an article dated 1999, Capitol Hill Blue records that it contacted Miss Wellstone who confirmed the incident, but refused to discuss the matter further. She said she would not go public with further details of the attack. Later she changed her phone number and hired a barrister who warned a reporter to stay away from his client.

Both Bill Clinton and Cliff Jackson, the fellow Arkansan who helped him dodge the draft, were members of the Oxford University basketball B team. Jackson recalled that: 'Women weren't supposed to stay in the rooms overnight. And yet I know that during that period he had a woman living with him in his room at University College! She was an Indian, from India, that is. I remember meeting her and his telling me about it.' Clinton met Jackson later in life when he was campaigning to become president by which time the former friend had become 'a conservative Republican with a deep personal animosity towards me'.

Clinton had many other girlfriends whilst at Oxford. Katherine Veeker his 'part time lover' and daughter of a professor of philosophy regarded him as 'very cuddly and quite easily the most gregarious human being'. Whilst Tamara Eccles-Williams said that he was usually penniless 'but he was a very easygoing and a very caring person'. Another friend, Sara Maitland, said that his 'room at Univ was easily accessible and the college porter adored him. It was just, "Oh, yes, go on in!" It was all sort of looking the other way. Bill was to have all the rules broken. It was dead impressive.'

He took Sara Maitland and Mandy Merck to a lecture in Oxford by Germaine Greer, the archfeminist of those times who was then working on her book *The Female Eunuch* (1970). Lured by the prospect of a talk about sex from a six foot tall woman 'with great legs', Clinton was appalled by her central thesis that middle class men were no good at sex. According to Maitland, Greer claimed that 'intelligent women would only do it with lorry drivers.' At the end of the talk no one dared ask a question until Clinton got to his feet asking, 'In case you ever decide to give bourgeois men another chance, can I give you my phone number?' Greer declined.

Girls aside, Clinton was politically active during his stay in Oxford. In his first term at Oxford the Union passed a motion claiming that 'American democracy has failed' by 266 to 233 votes. But Clinton was not anti-American. At a discussion held in the Junior Common Room at Balliol College he stated to a mocking audience that, 'In the end democracy usually made the right choices.' *The Washington Times* reported that he organised and led an anti-war demo on October 15, 1969. A month afterwards more than 500 people marched on the US Embassy in London with Clinton acting as a marshal, while in Washington over 500,000 protestors marched on the White House on the same day.

Finally the Oxford adventure was over. He returned to the United States in 1970 and at Yale pursued his law degree to completion and met the lady who became his first lady – Hilary Rodham. Once qualified, he went to his home state to become a professor at the University of Arkansas. Within a year his political aspirations came to the fore when he stood, unsuccessfully, as a congressman. In 1975, he married Hilary, and the very next year was elected unopposed to the position of Attorney General of Arkansas. Just two years later he became governor of the state at the age of thirty-two – the youngest in the country. Rapid promotion indeed. However, this did not impress those whom he had left behind in Oxford. Returning for a visit to his old college soon after his election he was greeted by the college porter, a character named Douglas Millin, with the words, 'I hear you've become king of a place with two men and a dog.' And one of his tutors at Oxford, Sir Maurice Shock, is said to have remarked that Mr. Clinton would never have become governor of 'a very serious state'.

In 1980 he was voted out of office, making him in his own words 'the youngest ex-governor in the nation's history'. But he bounced back two years later to become governor for the next ten years. It was during this period that the Clintons became financially involved in the Whitewater Development Corporation, a connection that dogged the early years of his presidency.

Though Clinton did not gain an Oxford degree as a student, he did well for himself. Having shown the 'moral force of character and instincts to lead, and to take an interest in one's fellow beings' he gained the Presidency of the United States in 1992 (the third youngest man ever to do so and the first Oxonian). Consequently he was presented with an honorary degree from Oxford University in 1994. The campaign for the presidency was tough with many references to his sojourn in Oxford including the famous complaint that he had been 'tainted' by Oxford debating skills i.e. that he was too clever by half. He had a beard and longish hair during his second year in the city, so there were suggestions that he had been a dope-taking drop-out hippie and an unpatriotic subversive. There's a wonderful contradictory quotation by George Cawkwell, the Dean of Graduates at University College at the time of his stay: 'Mr. Clinton was an amiable person whose record at the college was absolutely impeccable. Mr Clinton did not strike me as some hairy horror or he certainly would not have been a member of my dining club.'

His election elicited plaudits from the establishment. Professor John Albery, master of University College, was 'totally delighted' that an old member of the college had been elected President of the United States. And the professor and fellows celebrated next day with a champagne breakfast in the master's lodging. Then came a difficult decision. Professor Albery proposed flying the Stars and Stripes from the college flagpole, in fact he proposed flying the college flag above the American flag in the way that the British Navy once did when they had captured a French frigate. Admitting that the idea was a 'rather naughty concept' he was persuaded that Americans might be offended by the display, given their well known sensitivity towards the American flag. The dean of University College, David Bell, argued against flying the American flag at all, saying it would demonstrate that 'We have buckled down to the USA.' He proposed that the college erect another flag pole just for the day so that the University College flag could be flown at a height equal to that of the American flag. Ultimately, the Stars and Stripes flew alone.

There were other reasons to celebrate that day. Clinton's election would hopefully bring an end to the succession of people who snooped around the college during the presidential campaign, 'disagreeable people, probably Republicans,' stated Professor Albery. Furthermore, Clinton's victory settled a score. 'George Bush tried to make Oxford a dirty word,' Professor Albery said.

Clinton's two terms as president were characterised by economic expansion, technological progress and social reform. However, they were also marred by accusations of dubious property dealing and antics in the White House with a certain Monica Lewinsky – the latter resulting in impeachment proceedings and a new interpretation of the term 'sexual relations'. Yet for all his antics, or perhaps because of them, Clinton finished his second term with the highest approval rating of any president since World War II. He also brought a new look to the presidency through his use of the media, including playing saxophone on The Arsenio Hall Show (prompting the host to quip, 'It's nice to see a Democrat blow something besides the election').

Clinton remains popular with many throughout the world. In his own words, 'I may not have been the greatest president, but I've had the most fun eight years.' Perhaps it is the fun that people remember. The online publication of the Starr report which contains detailed evidence of his sexual encounters with Lewinsky almost flattened the Internet and promoted the humble cigar from a good smoke to a titillating dildo. Many also remember his responses during the impeachment proceedings where he claimed that because certain acts were performed on him, not by him, he did not engage in sexual relations – thereby strengthening the appropriateness of his nickname: 'Slippery Willie'. The impeachment proceedings were not successful.

Like Clinton, Lewinsky came to Oxford, but in her case it was not to study. She came to the city to promote and sign copies of the book *Monica's Story* (1999), written by Princess Diana's biographer Andrew Morton. Later, in 2006, she did come to England as a student. At the age of thirty-two, she received her Master of Science degree in Social Psychology from the London School of Economics. In his autobiography which appeared in 2004 the ex-president is fairly contrite about the whole affair with Lewinsky. After publication of the Starr Report he called his cabinet together and apologized to them. Reflecting on their reaction he wrote, 'I really understood for the first time the extent to which the exposure of my misconduct and dishonesty about it had opened a Pandora's Box of emotions in the American people.' Lewinsky was not impressed. In an interview with the *Daily Mail* she said, 'He could have made it right with the book, but he hasn't. He is a revisionist of history. He has lied.'

Throughout his life Oxford seems to have had an almost magnetic attraction for Clinton. In 1973 he brought Hilary to the city for her first visit; it was during the same trip that he proposed to her in the romantic surroundings of the Lake District (she turned him down). In 1994 he returned to Oxford to collect his honorary degree, and in 2001 to open the Rothermere American Institute, a centre of American study within Oxford University. In that same year his daughter, Chelsea, graduated with distinction from Stanford University; her undergraduate thesis being based on her father's mediation of the 1998 Northern Ireland peace agreement. Following this she came to Oxford as a postgraduate, to her father's old college in fact, and of course Daddy came to visit her, showing her the rooms where he had stayed in his first year, pointing out the windowsill where he stored milk in winter to keep it fresh.

Though Chelsea earned a Master's degree in international relations, the newspapers reported that she was not too happy in the city. In her own words, 'It's hard to be abroad right now.

Every day I encounter some sort of anti-American feeling. Sometimes it's from other students, sometimes it's from a newspaper columnist, sometimes it's from "peace" demonstrators.' Earlier that year her father had faced a similar reaction as he walked through the streets of Oxford to the Rothermere Institute. When he was harangued by a young student over the deaths of thousands of Iraqis during his presidency. He responded by saying, 'Saddam Hussain spent millions on building himself a palace when he could have spent it on his people.'

There was a rumour that Chelsea might transfer to the London School of Economics. This produced a response from local radio station Fusion FM. They launched a *Cheer up Chelsea Day*, playing American music and 'flooding the airwaves with words of encouragement'. She stayed and her father came to Oxford in 2003 to witness his daughter presenting her thesis to the university. He, ever perky, is quoted as saying, 'She got her degree – so we've got now two Oxford educations and one degree. I got an honorary degree but she's now redeemed the family honour by finishing her degree.'

During Bill Clinton's first presidential campaign, I recall that there was the traditional digging into his early life, especially concerning the women that he had known. When asked what she thought of the allegations that were beginning to surface, Hilary said something to the effect that she knew she wasn't his first lady but she was very much looking forward to being the First Lady. In 2008 she ran as a candidate to be the Democrat nominee for president. I wonder how our Oxford rogue, Bill Clinton, would have taken to being the First Man of the first female president. The signs are that he would have been his usual charming self; he even called himself a prospective 'First Laddy' in waiting. However, his wife did not win the candidacy.

Bill Clinton's own summary of the two years at Oxford is telling – he calls them 'the most extraordinary years of my life'. Given the extraordinary nature of the life that followed, they must have been extraordinary indeed!

Rogue Assessment:

| | | | | | | | |
|---|---|---|---|---|---|---|---|
| Charmer | [ ] | Womaniser | [ ] | Drinker | [ ] | Liar | [ ] |
| Entertainer | [ ] | Corrupter | [ ] | Adventurer | [ ] | Creator | [ ] |

Sources:
*My Life* by Bill Clinton. Hutchinson, 2004
*Bill Clinton. An American Journey* by Nigel Hamilton, Century 2003
*Mr Nice* by Howard Marks. Minerva, 1997.
*'All the President's victims III'*. Capitol Hill Blue, 2007
*Unlimited Access* by GaryAldritch. Regnery Publishing, 1998.
'Bill Clinton' Wikipedia biography, 2008
*Clinton: 'The luck of the Welsh'*. BBC News report. 27 May, 2001
*'Oxford Elated (in Its Fashion) Over Clinton'*. New York Times, August 11, 2008
*The President We Deserve by Martin Walker.* Crown Publishers, 1996

# THE POET
## Percy Shelley
*1792-1822*

The trail returns to the High from Magpie Lane, turns right, passing the old bank which is now a swish restaurant and hotel, and encounters the beginnings of the long frontage of University College. This is the first college to have been founded in Oxford back in 1249. In times gone by it claimed an even earlier foundation and a grand founder – Alfred the Great. This mythical origin was abandoned in 1872 when the Regius Professor of History sent the college a plate of burnt cakes to mock its putative millennium. It remains the most secretive of the central colleges, keeping its door shut against all but the most persistent, or qualified, of visitors.

Look for the plaque in the High on the front wall of Univ. The plaque has nothing to do with the college itself: it simply celebrates the residency of Robert Boyle who, during the 1650s, had lodgings in a house here. It was in this house that he discovered Boyle's Law, which all good schoolchildren learn by heart. However, the house has long gone and behind the wall is a rotunda capped with a lead dome – clearly visible if you stand on the other side of the road. Beneath that dome lies the elegant, reclining statue of our next rogue – Percy Bysshe Shelley.

Shelley was born of the moneyed aristocracy – his father was Sir Timothy Shelley, a member of parliament, and his grandfather the first Baronet Shelley of Castle Goring, Sussex. The odd name Bysshe (sometime Bysse) derives from a wealthy lady called Helen Bysshe who brought the Bysshe estate to the Shelley family in the seventeenth century. It is pronounced as bishop without the 'op'.

Shelley was a girlish-looking boy and he suffered for that. Both at his prep school and at Eton, he was persistently bullied and could do little to protect himself. As one of his classmates wrote, he was 'like a girl in boy's clothes, fighting with open hands'. Having already acquired the title 'Mad Shelley' through his eccentricity at Eton, he came up to University College in 1810.

There are many stories of his strange behaviour here, some of which must surely be true! It is said that he electrified the front door of the college, which may well accord with the view that he was not popular with either other students or the dons. On the other hand he constructed a still in his room to produce alcohol – which should have increased his popularity. Then there is the odd tale of the babies. From the main entrance of Univ Shelley could look over the High to the shops opposite, one of which was the bookshop of Slatter and Munday that was to have a pivotal role in his departure from Oxford. In those days mothers were far more trusting than today and would happily leave their babies in perambulators outside shops whilst they shopped inside. Shelley would wait until a reasonable collection of prams had been assembled, then walk across the High and swop the babies around before returning to the college entrance to watch the confusion!

There was another baby incident. Whilst crossing Magdalen Bridge with his friend Thomas Hogg, deep in a dispute on the arcane subject of reincarnation, he snatched a baby from its mother's arms. Dandling the poor child above the river he cried out, 'Can your baby tell us about pre-existence, Madam?' It could not, and the mother was very relieved to retrieve her baby from the crazy youngster.

These are the tales that tour leaders entertain their groups with as they speak of Shelley in the shadow of his old college. They may well be true, some of the events are underwritten to some extent by this endearing description of Shelley's room at Univ, as described by his friend Thomas Hogg:

> Books, boots, papers, shoes, philosophical instruments, clothes, pistols, linen, crockery, ammunition, and phials innumerable, with money, stockings, prints, crucibles, bags, and boxes, were scattered on the floor in every place. ... The tables, and especially the carpet, were already stained with large spots of various hues, which frequently proclaimed the agency of fire. An electrical machine, an air-pump, the galvanic trough, a solar microscope, and large glass jars and receivers, were conspicuous amidst the mass of matter.

This scene is quite unlike the mental picture many people carry of Shelley the poet. This is more like the room of a mad scientist. Yet the 'electrical machine', no doubt a generator, would be capable of electrifying the front door and the 'glass jars and receivers' could well have formed the basis for a still.

He was certainly not an amiable student, though he did hold the odd party, inviting select students to 'wine and poetry in my room'. He hated dining in the hall and was the first to leave morning chapel (then compulsory). This eccentric young man attended very few lectures during his stay – some say only one – and established his own strange timetable, quite at odds with the general life of the college. He frequently read for sixteen hours a day, sleeping like an animal curled up on the hearthrug between six and ten in the evening, then rising to talk to Hogg whilst performing

University College with Shelley's dome

his chemical experiments throughout the night. Maybe he would have been happier in the unconstrained environment that Howard Marks enjoyed; certainly he grew his hair very long in contrast to the 'crew-cut' that was fashionable at the time. He railed against authority and Thomas Hogg stimulated and supported his railings.

Hogg was a stocky young man, in sharp contrast to Shelley's tall effeminacy. They met at one of the few detested dinners that Shelley actually did attend, began to discuss, found themselves kindred spirits, and continued the discussion until dawn in Shelley's room. And so began a lifelong friendship sometimes dotted with disastrous consequences yet resulting in Thomas Hogg becoming Shelley's biographer.

It seems that Hogg was Shelley's only close friend during his stay at Oxford. They walked out to the countryside on those afternoons which were not spent in furious study. Hogg likens the pair of them to Don Quixote and Sancho Panza – Shelley taking the part of the crazy knight – experiencing odd adventures in their wanderings. The budding poet often carried loaded pistols. He practiced with them by lodging letters from his father in a tree, aiming for the circular parliamentary franking mark – hardly a sign of filial loyalty or respect for authority. They trespassed in a secret garden, watched a boy beating a donkey, were attacked by a dog and indulged in the age-long pursuit of ducks and drakes – skimming stones across the mere below Shotover Hill. Shelley had a lifelong affinity with water and it was on these outings that he stretched Hogg's patience to the utmost by sailing paper boats across the mere and any other pond that he could find. Legend suggests that the paper boats also crossed the small lake which is now part of the Kilns where C.S. Lewis lived.

But it was reading that took up much of Shelley's time. Hogg once observed, 'If I were to read as long as you read, Shelley, my hair and teeth would be strewed about on the floor, and my eyes would slip down to my cheeks.' Yet there was time to write. During his first year he published a gothic novel entitled *Zastrozzi* (1810) and two collections of poetry, one with his sister.

Shelley looked forward to a long stay at Oxford. Thomas Hogg recalled this telling statement: 'I regret only that the period of our residence is limited to four years; I wish they would revive, for our sake, the old term of six or seven years. If we consider how much there is for us to learn.' Yet after less than a year he and Hogg had been expelled. This was nothing to do with the electrified door, or the babies, or the avoidance of lectures. What brought about the university's wrath was the publication of an anonymous pamphlet – *The Necessity of Atheism* (1811). Producing anonymous pamphlets that questioned authority and stirred up debate was a practice that he had already mastered at Eton.

Shelley's extreme distaste for deistic religion can be compared with that of the modern day Professor of Public Understanding of Science at Oxford – Richard Dawkins. But in Shelley's day atheism was certainly not to the taste of a university that demanded religious conformance from all of its members. Right up until the year of 1877 entrants had to sign the Thirty-Nine Articles in acceptance of the Church of England. Shelley and Hogg would certainly have signed.

The *Necessity of Atheism* was displayed in Slatter and Munday's directly opposite the college and sent, anonymously of course, to all of the bishops and heads of college. Within twenty minutes it had been spotted in the shop window by a fellow of New College who demanded that all copies be immediately burned. And the frightened proprietors complied – a single copy of the offending pamphlet being retained as evidence for the university authorities who were soon onto the case.

The shops opposite University College

Despite the anonymity, the revolutionaries were quickly traced and Shelley was called before the master and fellows of University College. There are many versions of what exactly was said here though one quote from Shelley via Hogg suggests that the poet became extremely heated, saying 'I have experienced tyranny and injustice before, and I well know what vulgar violence is; but I never met with such unworthy treatment.' In any event he did not admit to authoring the pamphlet and was sent down on the convenient accusation of 'contumacy in refusing to answer certain questions put to [him].' Convenient because it neatly avoided the debate on atheism.

Though Shelley clearly courted expulsion, Hogg's account of what followed indicates that he did not welcome it. He rushed straight to his friend's room and 'sat on the sofa, repeating with convulsive vehemence, the words, 'Expelled! Expelled!', his head shaking with emotion and his whole frame quivering'. Incensed by this cruel punishment the loyal Hogg marched to the master's lodgings to protest. As a result of that meeting he, the co-author of the dreaded pamphlet, was expelled for the same reasons as his friend. They were both sent down on March 25, 1811.

When Shelley's father was informed of the disaster he proposed two future courses: either Shelley returned to the family home to receive private lessons with tutors chosen by Sir Timothy or he would cut his son off – leaving him to 'the punishment and misery that belongs to a wicked pursuit of an opinion so diabolical and wicked as that which you have declared'. The son rejected both proposals and his intransigence, together with his father's fear of a public prosecution which might result from publication of the pamphlet, caused a permanent rift of such proportions that Sir Timothy would only communicate with his son through a solicitor. Shelley then proposed that he renounce his inheritance (a vast estate from his grandfather) for an annuity of £2000. This proposal shocked his father more than his son's avowed atheism – and was taken as a sure sign of his son's growing socialistic beliefs. An annuity of £200 was finally agreed upon without renouncing the inheritance, but with certain restrictions regarding the promotion of atheism. On these terms Shelley returned to the family home.

So far I have described a somewhat effeminate, fun-loving young man of principle, with just glimpses of roguery. However, Shelley was soon to surprise his father once more when he eloped to Scotland with a young woman whom he had met through his younger sister. Harriet

Westerbrook was just sixteen at the time, and Percy Shelley only nineteen. On the register he described himself as 'farmer, Sussex'.

Soon after the marriage Shelley suggested that his friend Hogg join them in an extended relationship: a *ménage à trois*. Harriet's views were not nearly as liberal as those of her young husband so Hogg was quickly displaced in the marital home by Harriet's thirty-year old sister. Some biographies record this differently, suggesting that Hogg tried to seduce Harriet whilst Shelley was absent and for that reason was replaced. With nearly thirty biographies of Shelley to choose from, there are many interpretations of the same event.

That Shelley was a believer in 'free love' is undoubted. He encouraged women to aspire to a greater freedom, to throw off the rules that civilisation imposed and to become more independent. However, one critic likens him to the hippies of the 1960s who confused sexual liberation with women's liberation. Whatever the truth of the matter, the Shelley entourage took to the road and the family expanded. A child was born and a new lady added to the group – Elizabeth Hitchener.

They travelled to Ireland where Shelley published pamphlets and gave speeches supporting Catholic emancipation and Irish autonomy. He became a vegetarian and he twice tried to establish communes of egalitarian sympathisers in Wales. Neither succeeded; the second, at Tremadoc, ended drastically when Shelley claimed that he was the subject of an assassination attempt.

It is easy to form a picture of Shelley as soft, poetic and vulnerable – but that would be wrong. The attack at Tremadoc was firmly resisted, though the assailant attempted to shoot the poet twice on the same stormy night. Shelley fought back, by his own account, with pistols, sword and wrestling. In fact he was very fond of pistols, carrying a pair on every outing at Oxford and, according to Hogg, handling them with 'inconceivable carelessness'. He was said to be 'much too ready' to use the guns, once threatening to shoot a dog in Oxford that had ripped his new blue coat and later in Italy using them to disperse a group of armed peasants.

Always on the move, at Lynmouth in Devon Shelley's entire 'family' was engaged in distributing his leaflet *The Declaration of Rights* (1812). In addition to flyposting, some ingenious means of distribution were employed: they sent leaflets up in hand-made hot air balloons and launched them into the Bristol Channel in bottles and small boats made of waxed boxes complete with sails.

Whilst at Oxford Shelley had read William Godwin's *Political Justice* (1793), which contained a critique of the laws of property and inheritance. He and the author entered into correspondence and, through this liaison, he became acquainted with Godwin's sixteen-year old daughter, Mary Wollstonecraft; and yes, you've guessed it, eloped with her. This time he went to France taking (you might have guessed this too) Mary's stepsister Claire Clairmont with him! A pattern seems to be emerging here. From Troyes he wrote affectionately to Harriet inviting her to join them! Harriet, who was pregnant with their second child at the time, declined.

Disgusted by his son's treatment of Harriet, Shelley's father cut off his allowance leaving the poet with serious debts. Then in 1816 Shelley's grandfather, the first Baronet, died and left him the very considerable income of £1000 per annum. Always short of money since his expulsion from Oxford, the poet was now rich and in the year of his grandfather's death Shelley made a trip with his new 'family' to Switzerland. Whilst travelling he had to state his occupation on hotel registers. What should he put? Poet perhaps? Actually, he entered the following: 'atheist, democrat, philanthropist'.

They rented a house near to Lord Byron's on the shores of Lake Geneva and conversation with Byron had a significant influence on Shelley's poetry, inspiring him to write 'Hymn to Intellectual Beauty' (1816). Byron was also an influence on Mary Shelley: it was at this time that she wrote *Frankenstein* (1818), which began as an entry for a game organised by Byron to determine who could write the best horror story.

At the end of the summer Shelley and Mary returned to England with Claire Clairmont, who was then pregnant with Byron's daughter. Tragedy awaited them: Mary's older half-sister, Fanny Imlay, committed suicide in the autumn, followed just a few months later by the death of Shelley's first wife, Harriet, who drowned herself in the Serpentine. Harriet's sad act allowed Shelley to marry Mary, which he did just a few weeks after the death.

The main poetic product of this period was 'The Revolt of Islam' (1817), in which Shelley attacked religion and which featured a pair of incestuous lovers. Following its publication the Shelleys travelled with Claire to Venice in order to introduce Byron to his new daughter, Allegra. The visit inspired Shelley once more. He wrote 'Julian and Maddalo' (1819) based on conversations with Byron, and 'Prometheus Unbound' (1819), a reconstruction of the lost Greek play. However, Italy was not a good place for Mary and Percy Shelley. Their son Will died of fever in Rome and their infant daughter Clara died during the journey to Byron's villa at Este. Fortunately there was some small relief from these two tragedies: another son, Percy Florence, was born in the city that provided his second name.

The Shelley family then moved to Pisa where the poet met Emilia Viviani, the nineteen-year old daughter of the governor of the city. This young lady had been consigned to a convent by her father while he tried to find her a suitable husband. Shelley met Emilia through a mutual acquaintance and became emotionally involved, entering into correspondence with her and writing *Epipsychidion* (1821), a long lyric poem which provides an overview of his search for ideal love. Could this relationship become number three in the series of elopements with young women? Possibly it might have, but Emilia was married off before things got to that point.

Shelley's political writing continued and in 1822 he founded a journal called *The Liberal* together with Byron and Leigh Hunt, the British poet and editor. This journal was to be the vehicle for their controversial and liberated ideals: an antidote to the English conservative press. Hunt was an old friend whom Shelley had brought over from England with his family at Byron's expense. Hunt's son provides a revealing glimpse of the characters of Byron and Shelley. He once had to undertake some errand that took him to Byron's room and found the great man feasting from a drum of figs. Byron offered him one, and he uses this event to contrast the two men. He recalled that Byron offered him a fig but 'Shelley would have handed me the drum and allowed me to help myself.'

In the event *The Liberal* was not to be, at least not for Shelley. In 1822 when the poet was just a month from his thirtieth birthday, he set sail from Livorno having welcomed Hunt to Italy. The journey was not expected to take long since Lerici where he was then living was only forty-five miles to the north. He was accompanied by his friend, Edward Williams (an ex-naval man), and a young English sailor, Charles Vivian. The three men were sailing Shelley's much-modified schooner – the Don Juan. Undecked, yet with no buoyancy aids, over-sailed and over-ballasted, it was by some accounts an accident waiting to happen. A sudden squall arose and the boat sank; sank so quickly that Williams did not have time to kick his boots off and Shelley thrust a book of poems by Keats so roughly into his pocket that it doubled back, splitting the spine.

The bodies of all three men were washed up on a beach near Viareggio ten days later, their faces so disfigured by fish bites as to be unrecognisable. Shelley was temporarily buried on the beach then later exhumed for cremation by a party of friends in an odd ceremony that saw Byron taking a swim in the sea. Parts of the body were removed as mementos (the heart was given to Mary while others took fragments of the 'curiously small' skull). Wine, oil, salt and frankincense were poured on the rotting cadaver, and once the flames had completed their work the ashes were taken to the Protestant Cemetery in Rome.

Perhaps it is not surprising that there are so many versions of Shelley's death – ranging from deliberate suicide to ramming by pirates. However, all the evidence points to a tragic accident caused by a heavy storm in combination with a boat that was not seaworthy. Added to this Shelley could not swim!

The Tory newspaper *The Courier* ungallantly reported the poet's death as follows: 'Shelley, the writer of some infidel poetry, has been drowned, now he knows whether there is a God or not.' This elicited a robust response from Byron: 'You were all brutally mistaken about Shelley, who was without exception the best and least selfish man I ever knew. I never knew anyone who was not a beast in comparison.'

Did Shelley fear death? Presumably. But he once wrote: 'How wonderful is death! Death and his brother sleep.' And now he had found rest, in his own words: 'He has outsoared the shadow of our night; envy and calumny and hate and pain, and that unrest which men miscall delight, can touch him not and torture not again; from the contagion of the world's slow stain, he is secure.' The poet was no more – he left behind his wife Mary, his son Percy Florence and the unfinished work 'The Triumph of Life'.

Though Shelley left University College in disgrace, he was welcomed back in 1893 when a beautiful statue of him was donated by his daughter-in-law, Lady Shelley. The college was not the first choice as repository for this fine white-marble statue, which shows the poet lying in a drowned position. It was originally intended for the Protestant Cemetery in Rome but was considered inappropriate. Nonetheless, there seems to be ironical justice in placing the memorial in what is now a secular college – the very college from which he was expelled after expressing an atheistic point of view. The statue, which lies beneath a specially constructed dome visible from the High, stands on a decorative plinth and is protected by iron railings. The latter are a later addition – to protect the poet from students who had a penchant for painting his fingernails and toenails red! Perhaps he would have smiled at this demonstration of youthful irreverence.

Some literary experts ladle unreserved praise on the works of Shelley stating that 'his lyric poems are superb in their beauty, grandeur and mastery of language'. He is sometimes called England's greatest romantic poet, and certainly this rogue remains a powerful poetic voice even in the twenty-first century. For all of that, the last word on Percy Shelley goes to a former professor of poetry, Matthew Arnold, once a student at Balliol and fellow of Oriel College. Arnold described the poet as 'a beautiful and ineffectual angel, beating in the void his luminous wings in vain'.

Rogue Assessment:

| | | | | | | | |
|---|---|---|---|---|---|---|---|
| Charmer | [ ] | Womaniser | [ ] | Drinker | [ ] | Liar | [ ] |
| Entertainer | [ ] | Corrupter | [ ] | Adventurer | [ ] | Creator | [ ] |

Sources:

*Percy Bysshe Shelley at Oxford* by Thomas Hogg. New Monthly Magazine, Volume 19, No. 544. April 28, 1832
*Shelley: The Pursuit* by Richard Holmes. Harper Collins, 1974
*Oxford in English Literature* by John Dougill. The University of Michigan Press, 1998
*Being Shelley* by Anne Wroe. Jonathan Cape, 2007
'Percy Bysshe Shelley.' Wikipedia biography, 2008
'Death and Destiny' by Richard Holmes. The Guardian Review, 2004
'Percy Bysshe Shelley Quotes.' Famous Poets and Poems.com

# The Rogue Male Trail

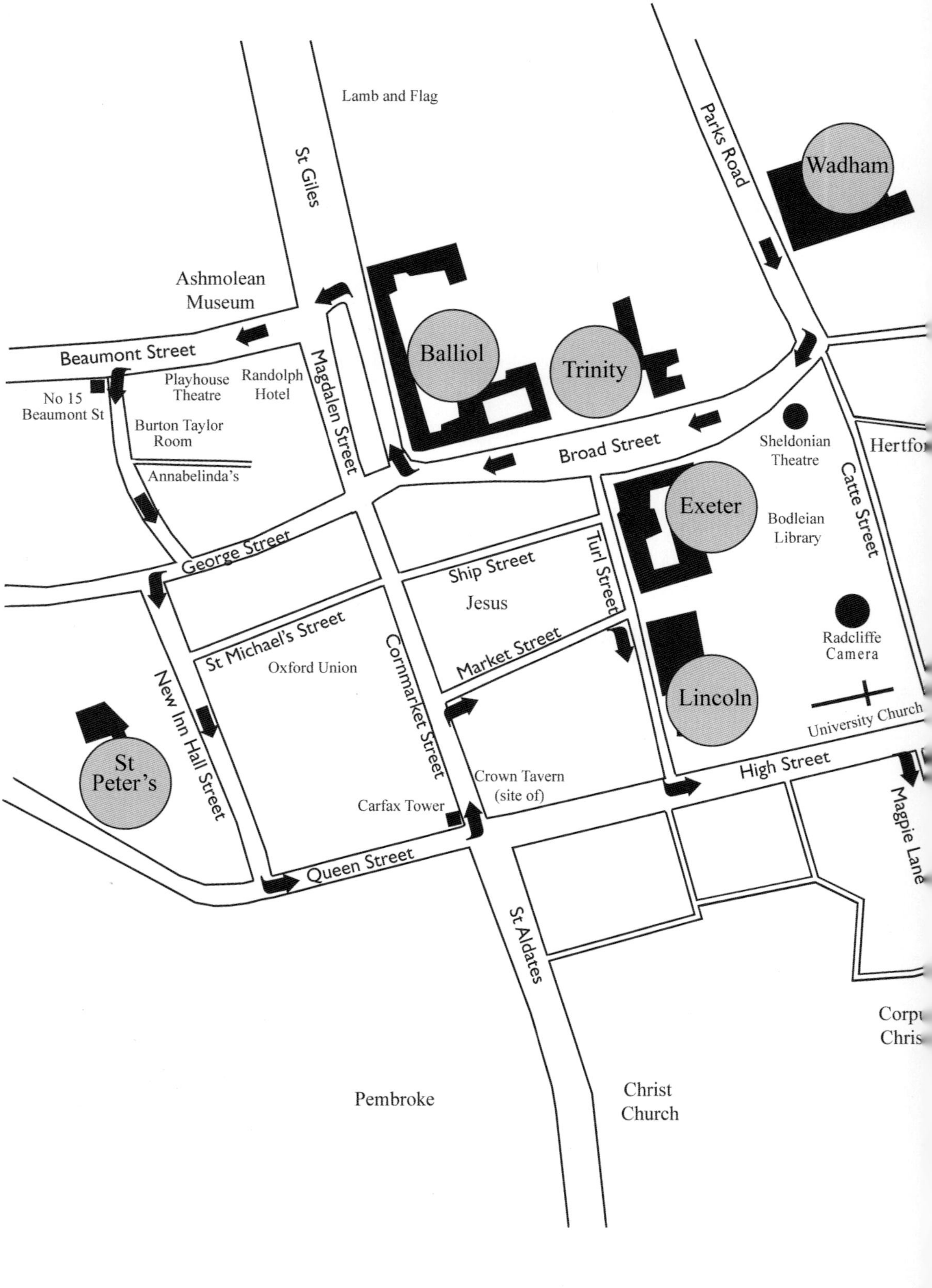

# Key

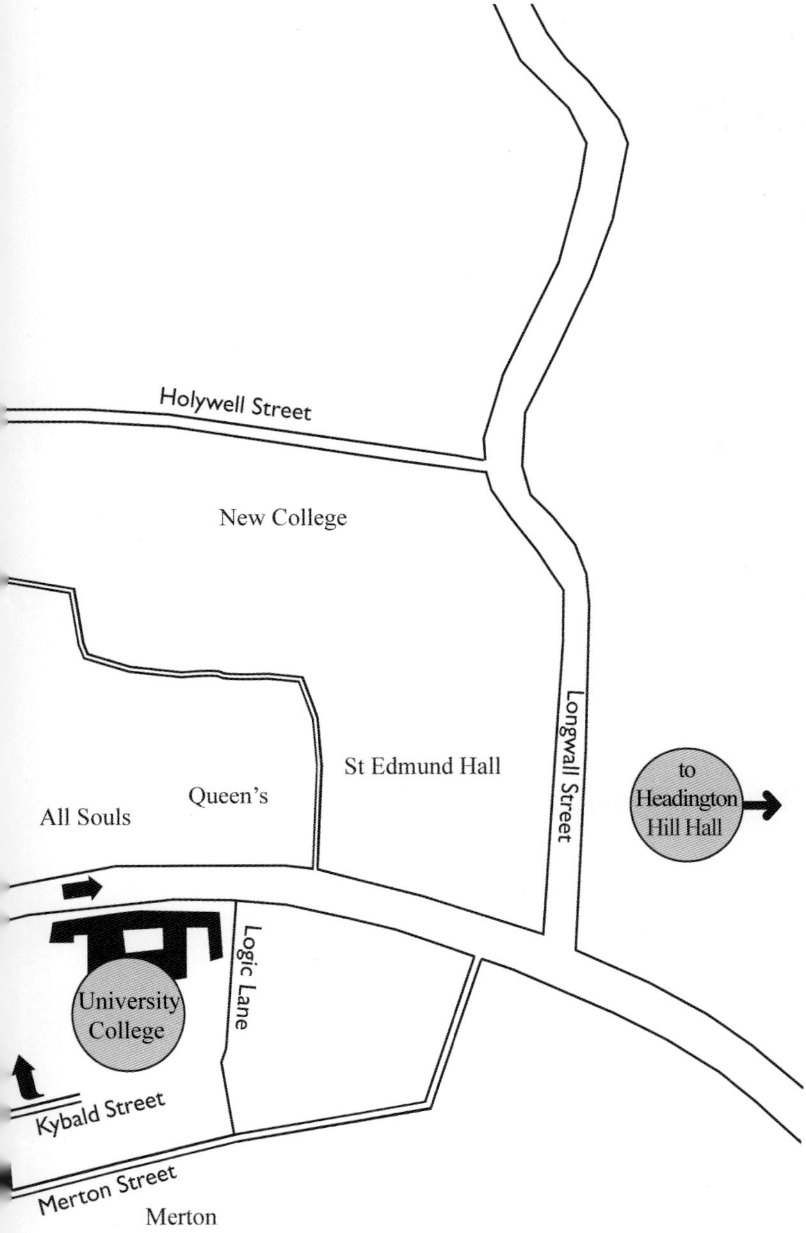


| | |
|---|---|
| Wadham | Lord Rochester |
| Exeter | Richard Burton |
| Trinity | Sir Richard Burton |
| Balliol | Graham Greene<br>Howard Marks |
| St Peter's | Richard Head |
| Lincoln | Sir William Davenant |
| Headington Hill Hall | Robert Maxwell |
| University College | Bill Clinton<br>Percy Shelley |

Oxface Publications
01865 723316
www.oxface.co.uk
info@oxface.co.uk

Other publications include:

*Oxford's Famous Faces*
by John Dougill

*Oxford: A Literary Guide*
by John Dougill